ARCHITECTURE

PERSPECTIVE

SHADOWS AND

REFLECTIONS

DIK VROMAN

VNR VAN NOSTRAND REINHOLD COMPANY
NEW YORK   CINCINNATI   TORONTO   LONDON   MELBOURNE

Library of Congress Catalog Card Number: 83-3524
ISBN: 0-442-28825-5
ISBN: 0-442-28826-3 pbk.

Manufactured in the United States of America

Published by Van Nostrand Reinhold Company Inc.
135 West 50th Street, New York, N.Y. 10020

Van Nostrand Reinhold
480 Latrobe Street
Melbourne, Victoria 3000, Australia

Van Nostrand Reinhold Company Ltd.
Molly Millars Lane
Wokingham, Berkshire, England

15 14 13 12 11 10 9 8 7 6 5 4 3 2 1

Library of Congress Cataloging in Publication Data

Vrooman, Dik.
   Architecture: perspective, shadows, and reflections.

   1. Architectural rendering--Technique. 2. Architec-
tural drawing--Technique. 3. Perspective. 4. Shades
and shadows. 5. Reflections. I. Title.
NA2780.V76 1983   720'.28'4   83-3524
ISBN 0-442-28825-5
ISBN 0-442-28826-3 pbk.

HOW DO WE DRAW, ACCURATELY AND QUICKLY, A PERSPECTIVE OF A DESIGN IDEA?

HOW DO WE CONSTRUCT EXACT SHADOWS DIRECTLY IN OUR PERSPECTIVE AFTER PLACING A PRINCIPAL SHADOW WHERE WE WANT TO SEE IT?

HOW DO WE CONSTRUCT EXACT REFLECTIONS DIRECTLY IN PERSPECTIVE?

AND HOW DO WE COMBINE SHADOWS, REFLECTIONS AND TRANSPARENCY — AS FOR WINDOWS — TO DRAW A REALISTIC PICTURE?

THIS BOOK ANSWERS THESE QUESTIONS IN DETAIL. INCLUDED ARE 3-POINT PERSPECTIVE AND ODD-ANGULAR AND CURVILINEAR FORMS. SHADOWS ARE EXPLAINED FOR BOTH THE SUN AND OTHER LIGHT SOURCES. REFLECTIONS ARE EXPLAINED FOR BOTH POOLS AND MIRRORS. THE CONSTRUCTION OF SCALE FIGURES AND TREES IS EXPLAINED. TEXTURES ARE SUGGESTED FOR RENDERING. FINALLY, THE CURVILINEAR ASPECT OF STRAIGHT-LINE PERSPECTIVE IS NOTED.

THIS BOOK IS FOR STUDENTS OF ARCHITECTURE, DESIGN AND ILLUSTRATION, AND FOR ANYONE ELSE WHO WANTS TO DRAW REALISTICALLY.

CONTENTS

WHAT WE SEE OR VISUALIZE, AND HOW TO DRAW IT

TO DRAW 3-DIMENSIONAL OBJECTS AS WE SEE THEM, WE MUST DRAW THEM IN PERSPECTIVE. IF AN OBJECT EXISTS, WE CAN PHOTOGRAPH IT, THEN TRACE THE PHOTOGRAPH FOR OUR PERSPECTIVE DRAWING. BUT IF WE ARE DESIGNING AN OBJECT WHICH DOES NOT YET EXIST, WE NEED TO KNOW HOW TO DRAW OUR IDEAS IN PERSPECTIVE. PLANS, SECTIONS AND ELEVATIONS ARE USEFUL IN THEIR WAYS, AND AXONOMETRICS APPROACH THE APPEARANCE OF AN OBJECT, BUT ONLY PERSPECTIVES TELL US HOW OUR DESIGN WILL REALLY BE SEEN.

PERSPECTIVE DRAWING SHOWS US THE SHAPE OF AN OBJECT. TO SEE THE OBJECT EVEN MORE REALISTICALLY, WE NEED TO DISTINGUISH BETWEEN LIGHT SURFACES AND SHADE AND SHADOW SURFACES, AND WE NEED TO INCORPORATE REFLECTIONS (BOTH CLEAR AND SUBTLE).

OF COURSE, APPROPRIATE LINE QUALITY (THIN OR THICK) AND EFFECTIVE VALUE CONTRASTS (LIGHT AREAS AGAINST DARK AREAS) ARE ALSO IMPORTANT FACTORS OF A GOOD DRAWING.

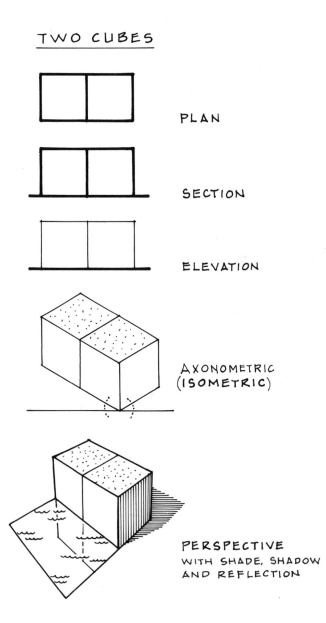

TWO CUBES

PLAN

SECTION

ELEVATION

AXONOMETRIC (ISOMETRIC)

PERSPECTIVE
WITH SHADE, SHADOW AND REFLECTION

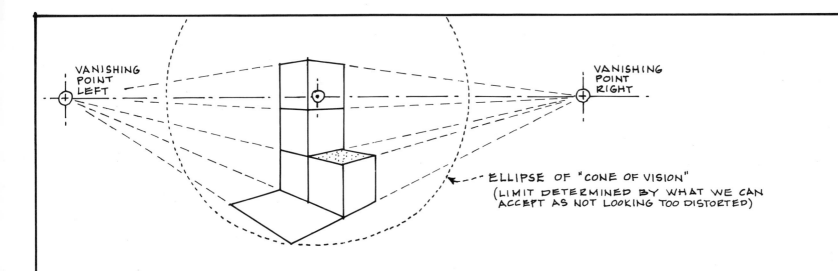

VANISHING POINT LEFT

VANISHING POINT RIGHT

ELLIPSE OF "CONE OF VISION"
(LIMIT DETERMINED BY WHAT WE CAN
ACCEPT AS NOT LOOKING TOO DISTORTED)

PERSPECTIVE DRAWING IS BASED ON THE OBSERVATION THAT LINES WHICH ARE ACTUALLY PARALLEL APPEAR TO CONVERGE TO A "VANISHING POINT." IN THIS SKETCH OF A RECTANGULAR FORM, THERE ARE TWO SUCH SETS OF LINES, SO WE HAVE "VANISHING POINT LEFT" AND "VANISHING POINT RIGHT." THE LINES OF THE THIRD SET IN THIS CASE REMAIN PARALLEL (ALL VERTICAL). THUS THIS IS KNOWN AS "TWO-POINT PERSPECTIVE."

WHEN WE ESTABLISH THESE TWO VANISHING POINTS ON THE HORIZON LINE, WE CAN PROCEED WITH THE DRAWING OF ALL HORIZONTAL RECTANGLES OR SQUARES WHICH ARE PARALLEL/ PERPENDICULAR TO THESE. (BUT IF WE ROTATED A RECTANGLE OR SQUARE AWAY FROM THIS RELATION, IT WOULD REQUIRE SEPARATE VANISHING POINTS LEFT AND RIGHT.)

A LITTLE "DRAMATIC DISTORTION" MAY BE EFFECTIVE, BUT IT CAN QUICKLY BECOME TOO MUCH IF WE TRY TO SEE BEYOND WHAT IS CALLED OUR "CONE OF VISION." PART OF THE PROBLEM IS THAT WE ASSUME THE "PICTURE PLANE" (ON WHICH WE MAKE OUR DRAWING) TO BE FLAT. WE ACCEPT THIS BECAUSE IT IS EASIER TO DRAW MECHANICALLY AN OBJECT RELATED TO FLAT PLANES AND STRAIGHT LINES.

ACTUALLY, THE PICTURE PLANE SHOULD BE CURVED (AS IS THE LENS OF THE EYE), BUT WE USUALLY LIMIT THE PICTURE WE DRAW TO THE CONE-OF-VISION AREA OF THE PAPER, AN AREA WHICH IS SO NEARLY FLAT THAT WE MAKE IT FLAT.

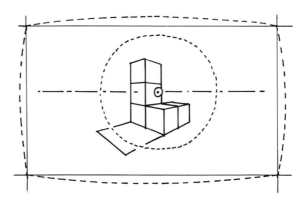

STUDY
№ 2

PAGE
7

PERSPECTIVE of OBSERVER'S PERSPECTIVE

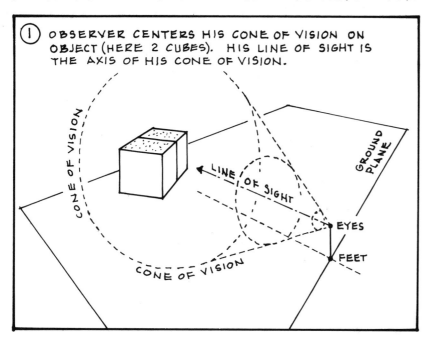

① OBSERVER CENTERS HIS CONE OF VISION ON OBJECT (HERE 2 CUBES). HIS LINE OF SIGHT IS THE AXIS OF HIS CONE OF VISION.

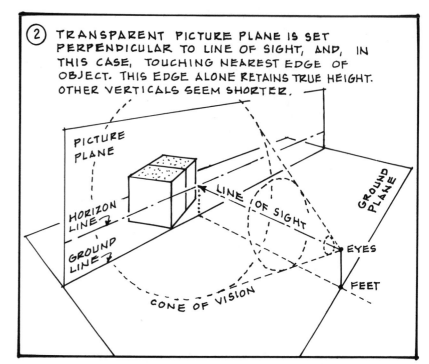

② TRANSPARENT PICTURE PLANE IS SET PERPENDICULAR TO LINE OF SIGHT, AND, IN THIS CASE, TOUCHING NEAREST EDGE OF OBJECT. THIS EDGE ALONE RETAINS TRUE HEIGHT. OTHER VERTICALS SEEM SHORTER.

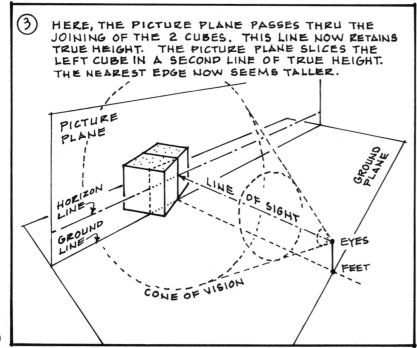

③ HERE, THE PICTURE PLANE PASSES THRU THE JOINING OF THE 2 CUBES. THIS LINE NOW RETAINS TRUE HEIGHT. THE PICTURE PLANE SLICES THE LEFT CUBE IN A SECOND LINE OF TRUE HEIGHT. THE NEAREST EDGE NOW SEEMS TALLER.

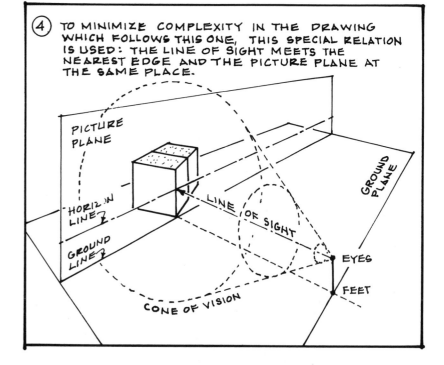

④ TO MINIMIZE COMPLEXITY IN THE DRAWING WHICH FOLLOWS THIS ONE, THIS SPECIAL RELATION IS USED: THE LINE OF SIGHT MEETS THE NEAREST EDGE AND THE PICTURE PLANE AT THE SAME PLACE.

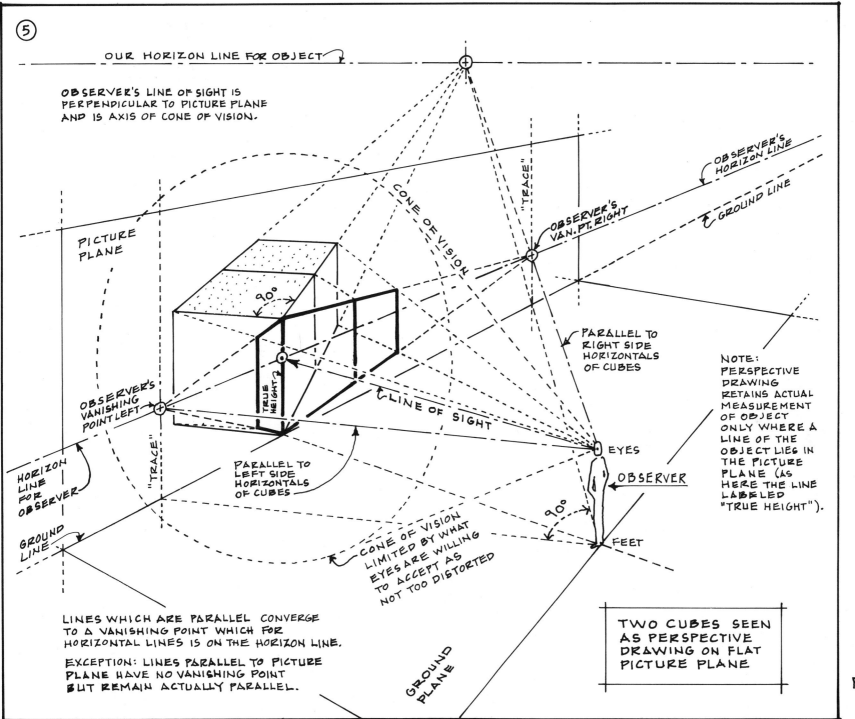

⑤

OUR HORIZON LINE FOR OBJECT

OBSERVER'S LINE OF SIGHT IS PERPENDICULAR TO PICTURE PLANE AND IS AXIS OF CONE OF VISION.

CONE OF VISION

"TRACE"

OBSERVER'S HORIZON LINE

OBSERVER'S VAN. PT. RIGHT

GROUND LINE

PICTURE PLANE

90°

PARALLEL TO RIGHT SIDE HORIZONTALS OF CUBES

NOTE: PERSPECTIVE DRAWING RETAINS ACTUAL MEASUREMENT OF OBJECT ONLY WHERE A LINE OF THE OBJECT LIES IN THE PICTURE PLANE (AS HERE THE LINE LABELED "TRUE HEIGHT").

TRUE HEIGHT

OBSERVER'S VANISHING POINT LEFT

LINE OF SIGHT

EYES

OBSERVER

HORIZON LINE FOR OBSERVER

"TRACE"

PARALLEL TO LEFT SIDE HORIZONTALS OF CUBES

90°

GROUND LINE

CONE OF VISION LIMITED BY WHAT EYES ARE WILLING TO ACCEPT AS NOT TOO DISTORTED

FEET

LINES WHICH ARE PARALLEL CONVERGE TO A VANISHING POINT WHICH FOR HORIZONTAL LINES IS ON THE HORIZON LINE.

EXCEPTION: LINES PARALLEL TO PICTURE PLANE HAVE NO VANISHING POINT BUT REMAIN ACTUALLY PARALLEL.

GROUND PLANE

TWO CUBES SEEN AS PERSPECTIVE DRAWING ON FLAT PICTURE PLANE

VARIOUS KINDS of PERSPECTIVE VIEWS of TWO JOINED CUBES

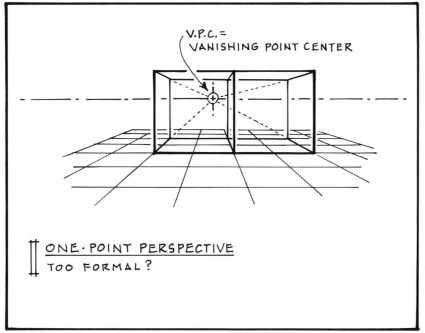

V.P.C. = VANISHING POINT CENTER

ONE·POINT PERSPECTIVE
TOO FORMAL?

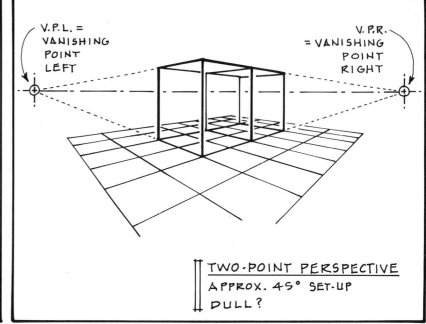

V.P.L. = VANISHING POINT LEFT

V.P.R. = VANISHING POINT RIGHT

TWO·POINT PERSPECTIVE
APPROX. 45° SET·UP
DULL?

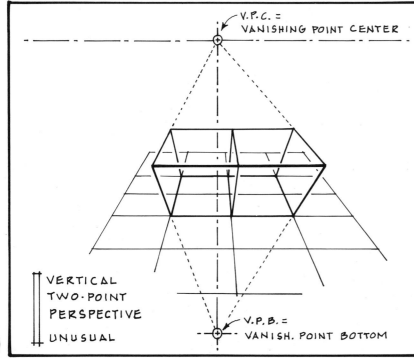

V.P.C. = VANISHING POINT CENTER

VERTICAL TWO·POINT PERSPECTIVE
UNUSUAL

V.P.B. = VANISH. POINT BOTTOM

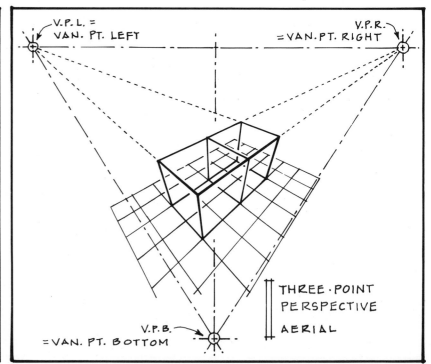

V.P.L. = VAN. PT. LEFT

V.P.R. = VAN. PT. RIGHT

THREE·POINT PERSPECTIVE
AERIAL

V.P.B. = VAN. PT. BOTTOM

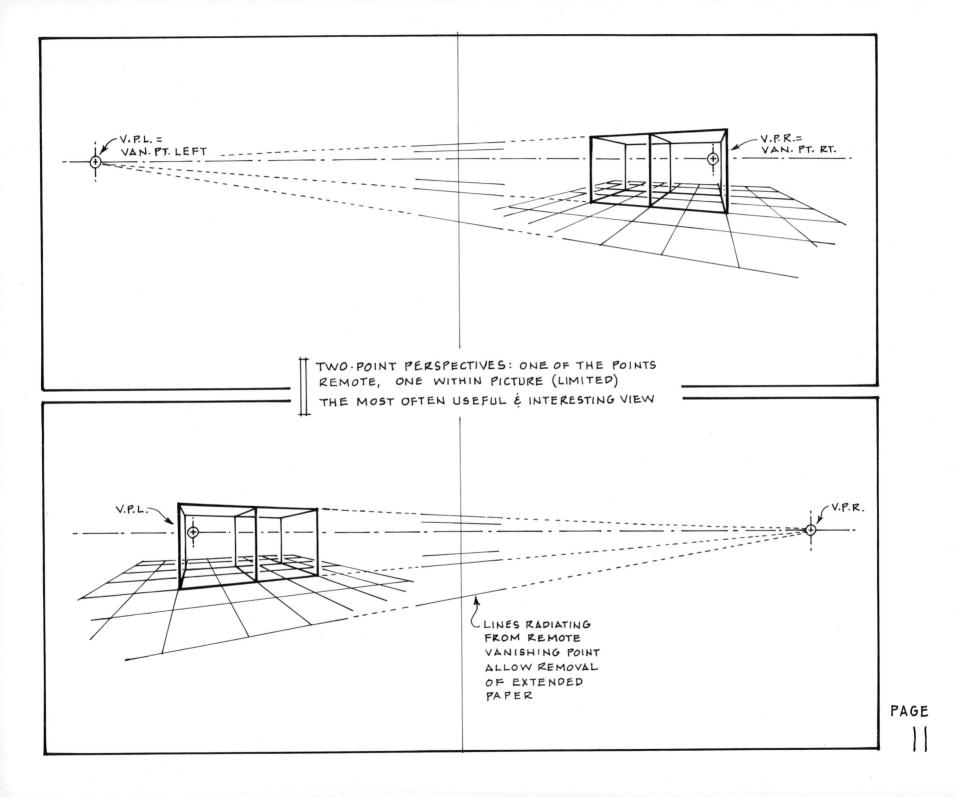

V.P.L. =
VAN. PT. LEFT

V.P.R.=
VAN. PT. RT.

TWO·POINT PERSPECTIVES: ONE OF THE POINTS
REMOTE, ONE WITHIN PICTURE (LIMITED)
THE MOST OFTEN USEFUL & INTERESTING VIEW

V.P.L.

V.P.R.

LINES RADIATING
FROM REMOTE
VANISHING POINT
ALLOW REMOVAL
OF EXTENDED
PAPER

PAGE
11

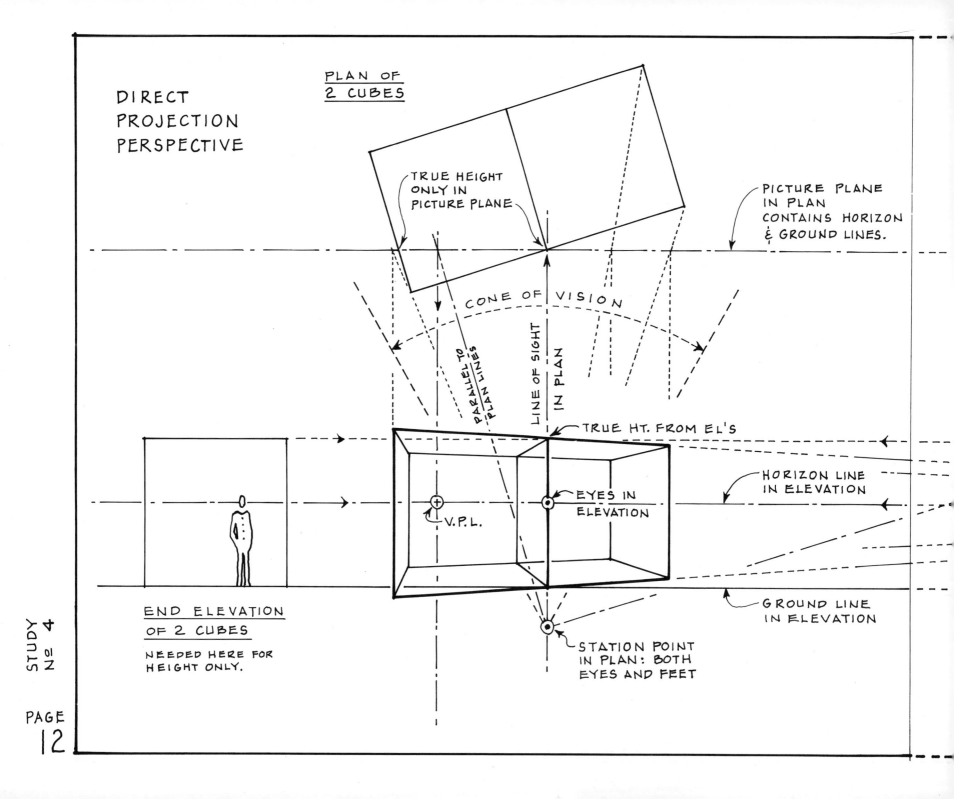

DIRECT
PROJECTION
PERSPECTIVE

PLAN OF
2 CUBES

TRUE HEIGHT
ONLY IN
PICTURE PLANE

PICTURE PLANE
IN PLAN
CONTAINS HORIZON
& GROUND LINES.

CONE OF VISION

PARALLEL TO PLAN LINES

LINE OF SIGHT IN PLAN

TRUE HT. FROM EL'S

HORIZON LINE
IN ELEVATION

EYES IN
ELEVATION

V.P.L.

END ELEVATION
OF 2 CUBES

NEEDED HERE FOR
HEIGHT ONLY.

GROUND LINE
IN ELEVATION

STATION POINT
IN PLAN: BOTH
EYES AND FEET

STUDY
Nº 4

PAGE
12

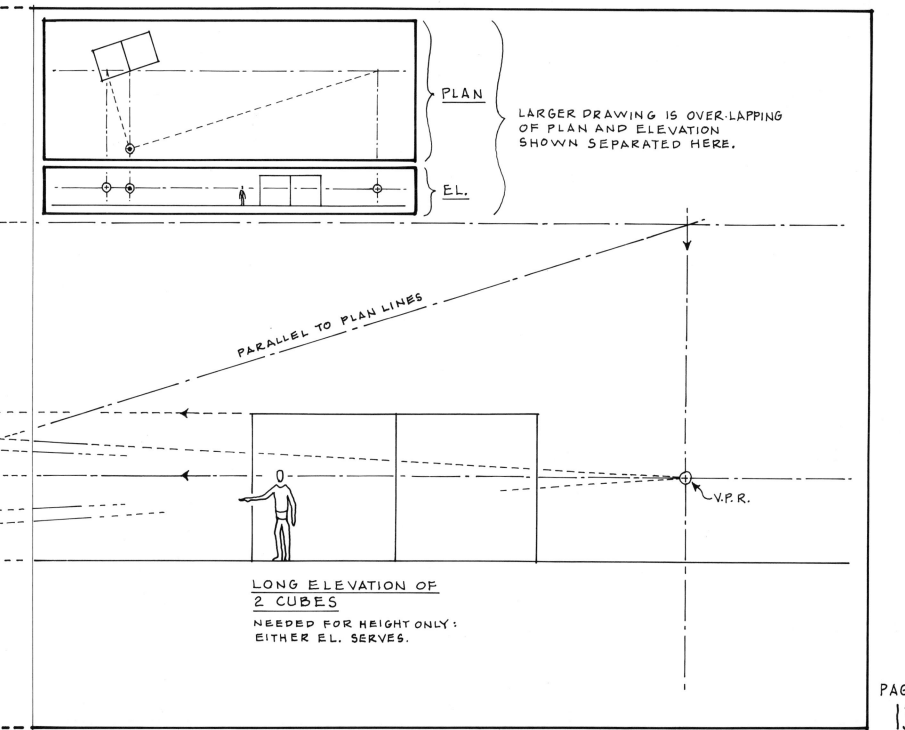

PLAN

EL.

LARGER DRAWING IS OVER-LAPPING
OF PLAN AND ELEVATION
SHOWN SEPARATED HERE.

PARALLEL TO PLAN LINES

V.P.R.

LONG ELEVATION OF
2 CUBES

NEEDED FOR HEIGHT ONLY:
EITHER EL. SERVES.

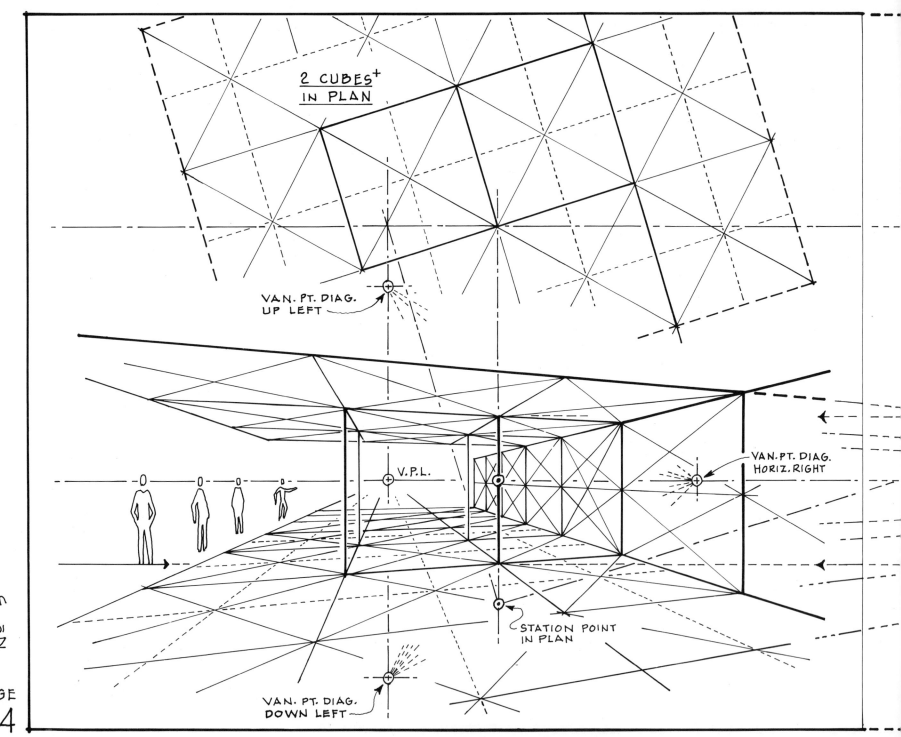

2 CUBES+
IN PLAN

VAN. PT. DIAG.
UP LEFT

VAN. PT. DIAG.
HORIZ. RIGHT

V.P.L.

STATION POINT
IN PLAN

VAN. PT. DIAG.
DOWN LEFT

STUDY
Nº 5

PAGE
14

EXTENSION of SQUARES and CUBES
BY USE of DIAGONALS

WITH "DIRECT PROJECTION" FOR CHECKING

(THIS MODULAR FRAMEWORK CAN ASSIST IN THE PERSPECTIVE
DRAWING OF MORE COMPLEX FORMS)

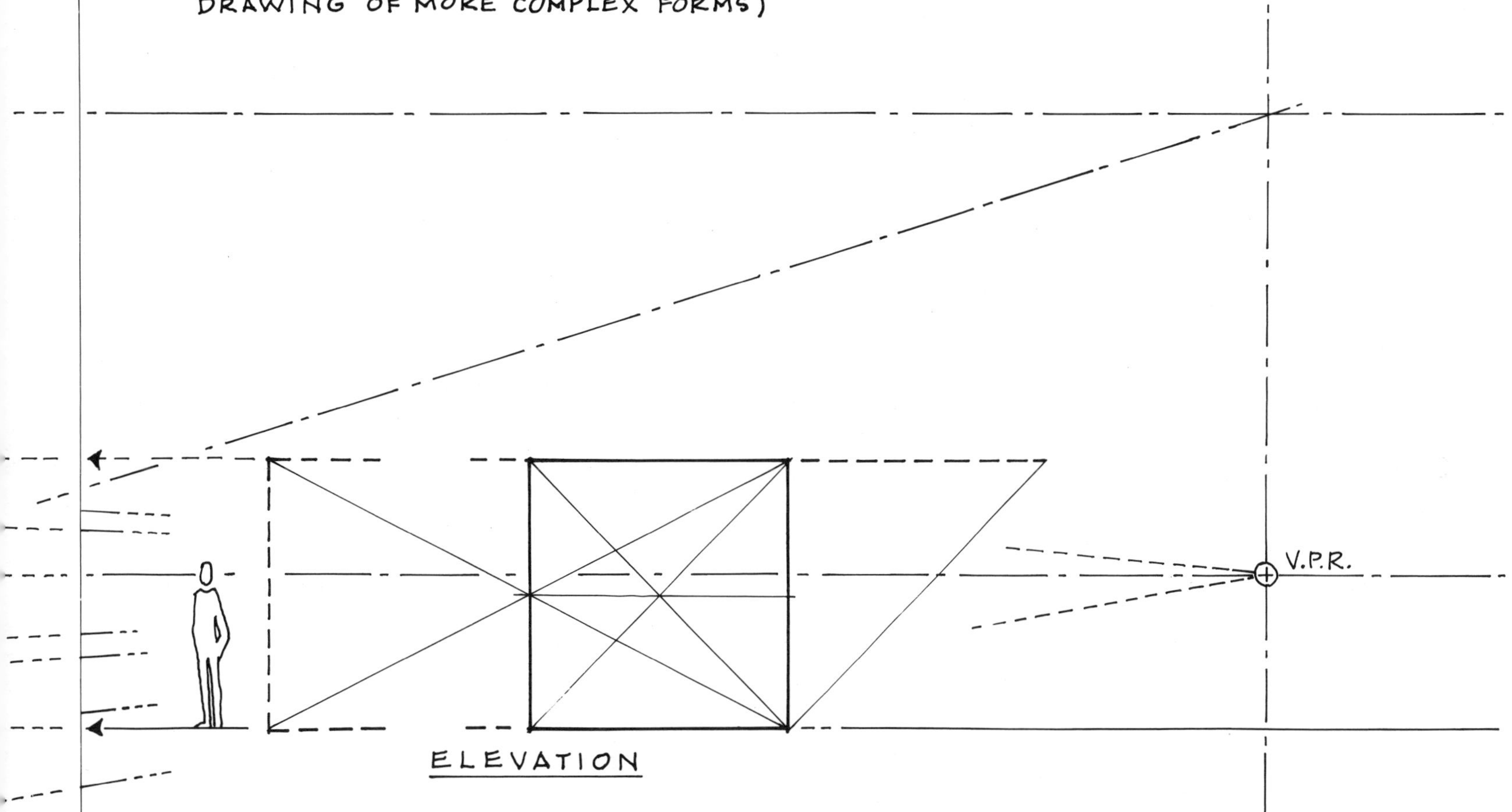

V.P.R.

ELEVATION

EXERCISE #1

DIRECT PROJECTION PERSPECTIVE: 2-POINT: NORMAL HORIZON

CUT AWAY THE NEXT SHEET AT DASHED LINE ⟶
TAPE THE SHEET TO YOUR DRAWING BOARD.

COMPLETE THE PERSPECTIVE DRAWING WITH MODIFICATIONS INDICATED IN ONE OF THESE VARIATIONS (A, B, C, OR D) AS ASSIGNED BY YOUR INSTRUCTOR.

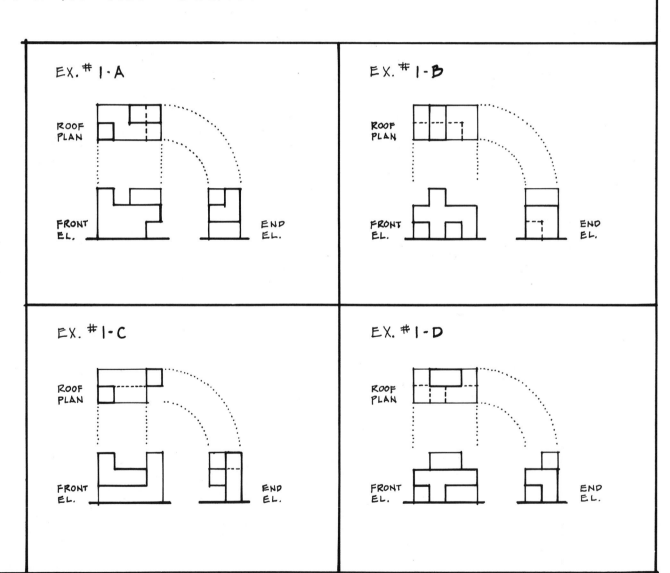

EX. #1-A

ROOF PLAN

FRONT EL.   END EL.

EX. #1-B

ROOF PLAN

FRONT EL.   END EL.

EX. #1-C

ROOF PLAN

FRONT EL.   END EL.

EX. #1-D

ROOF PLAN

FRONT EL.   END EL.

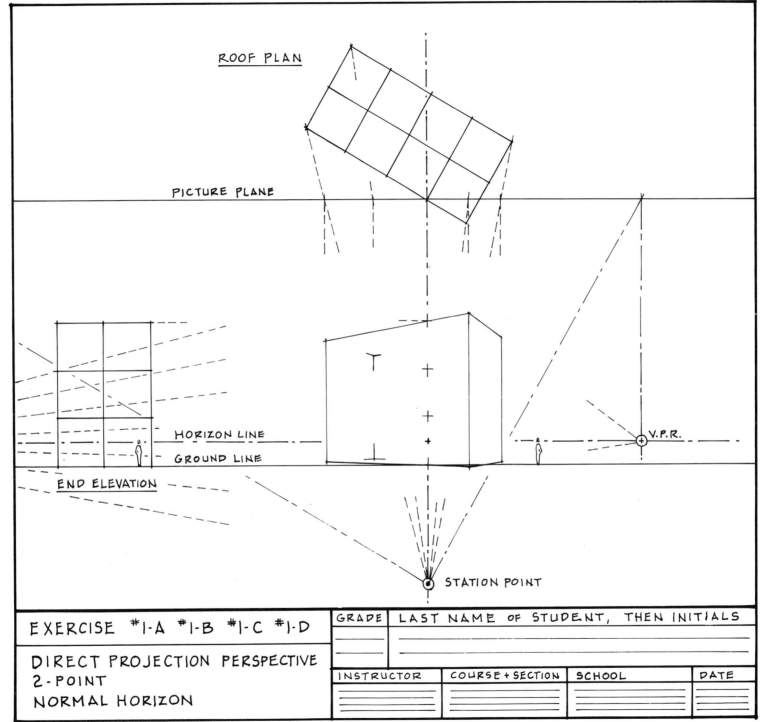

ROOF PLAN

PICTURE PLANE

HORIZON LINE
GROUND LINE

END ELEVATION

V.P.R.

STATION POINT

EXERCISE #1-A #1-B #1-C #1-D	GRADE	LAST NAME OF STUDENT, THEN INITIALS			
DIRECT PROJECTION PERSPECTIVE 2-POINT NORMAL HORIZON					
	INSTRUCTOR	COURSE + SECTION	SCHOOL	DATE	

DIRECT PROJECTION PERSPECTIVE: 2·POINT: HIGH HORIZON

TRACE EXERCISE #1, INCLUDING TITLE BOX (ADJUST THE INFORMATION), BUT CHANGE
THE HORIZON LINE TO BE LOCATED ONE SQUARE (OR STORY) ABOVE THE ROOF·TOP.
COMPLETE THE PERSPECTIVE.

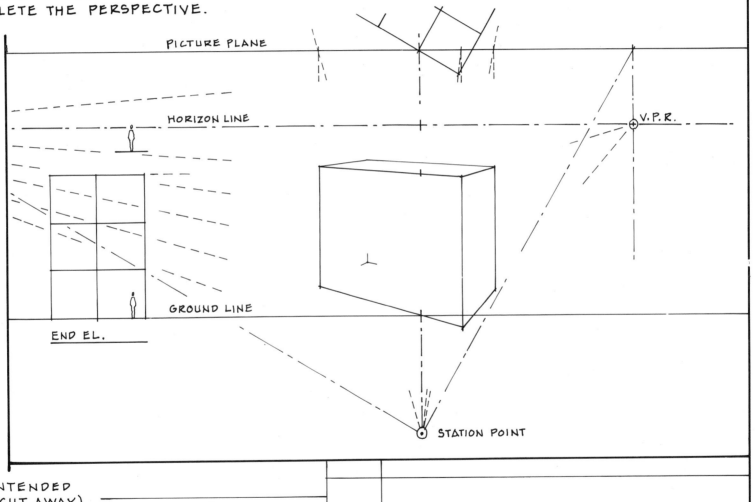

PICTURE PLANE

HORIZON LINE

V.P.R.

GROUND LINE

END EL.

STATION POINT

(NOT INTENDED
TO BE CUT AWAY)

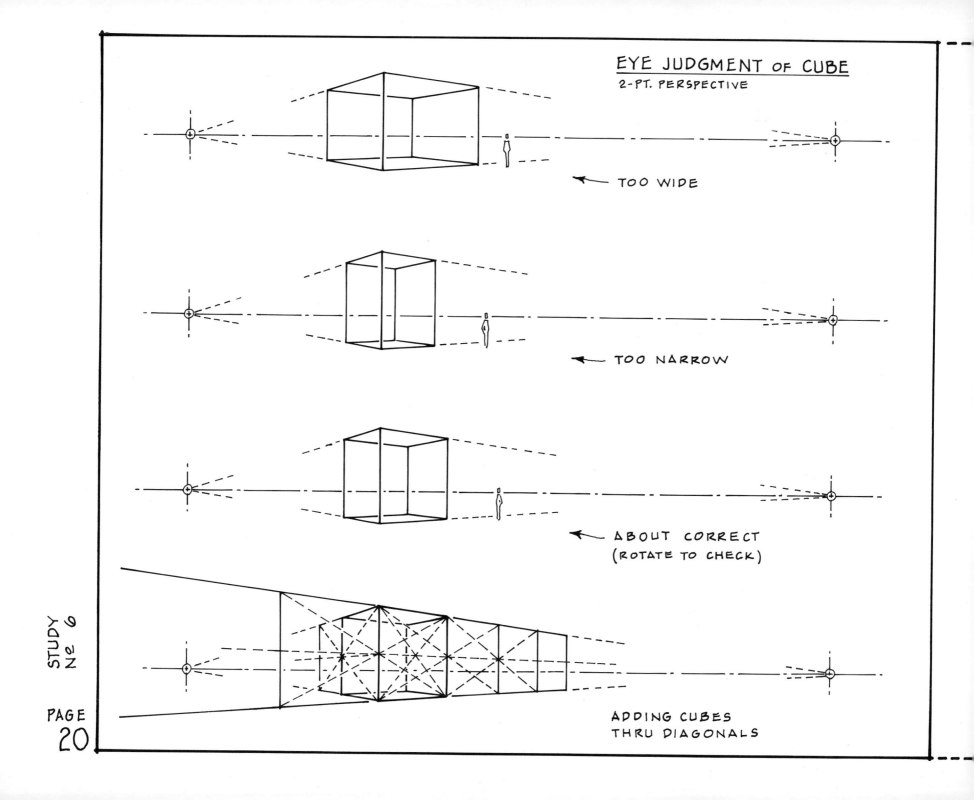

EYE JUDGMENT OF CUBE
2-PT. PERSPECTIVE

← TOO WIDE

← TOO NARROW

← ABOUT CORRECT
(ROTATE TO CHECK)

ADDING CUBES
THRU DIAGONALS

STUDY
№ 6

PAGE
20

CUBE-MODULE PERSPECTIVE DRAWING

WITHOUT DIRECT PROJECTION OF PLAN & ELEVATION

IF WE CAN "EYEBALL" A CENTRAL CUBE, THEN THRU DIAGONALS WE CAN EXPAND TO A "PENCIL SCAFFOLDING" OF CUBES, OUT OF WHICH WE CAN "CARVE" ANY PERSPECTIVE, RECTANGULAR, ODD-ANGULAR OR CURVILINEAR.
OUR BASIC CUBE SHOULD BE ASSIGNED A CONVENIENT DIMENSION.

EXAMPLE | BUILDING 40' LONG, 30' WIDE, 20' HIGH:
ONE | ASSUME A 10' CUBE MODULE (A CONVENIENT FACTOR):

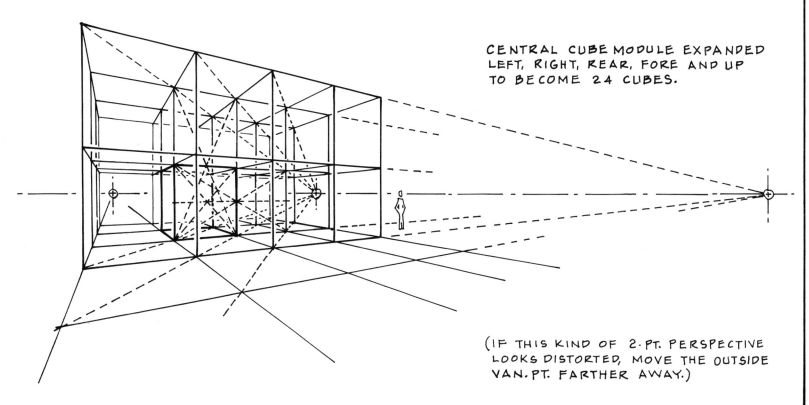

CENTRAL CUBE MODULE EXPANDED LEFT, RIGHT, REAR, FORE AND UP TO BECOME 24 CUBES.

(IF THIS KIND OF 2-PT. PERSPECTIVE LOOKS DISTORTED, MOVE THE OUTSIDE VAN. PT. FARTHER AWAY.)

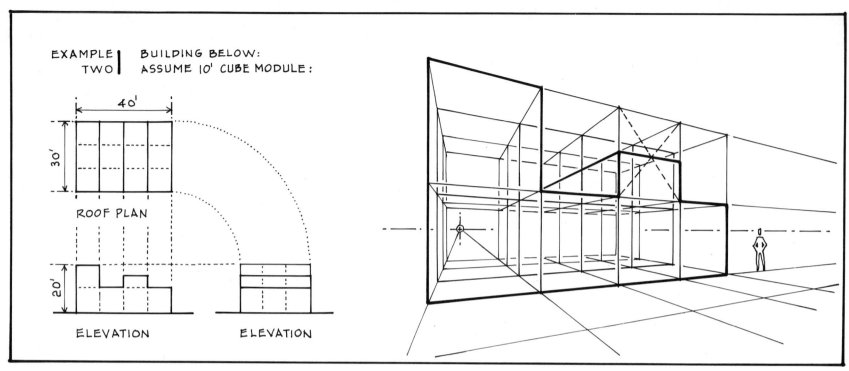

EXAMPLE TWO | BUILDING BELOW:
ASSUME 10' CUBE MODULE:

40'

30'

ROOF PLAN

20'

ELEVATION   ELEVATION

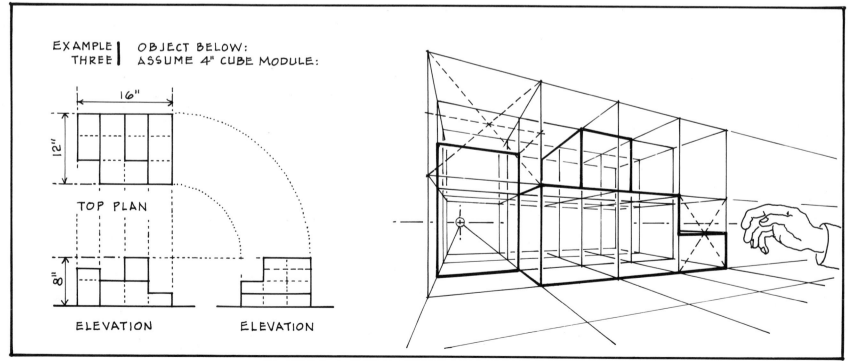

EXAMPLE THREE | OBJECT BELOW:
ASSUME 4" CUBE MODULE:

16"

12"

TOP PLAN

8"

ELEVATION   ELEVATION

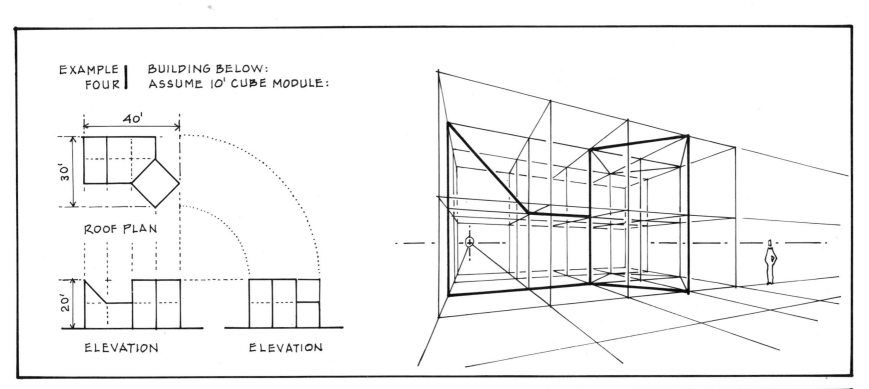

EXAMPLE FOUR | BUILDING BELOW:
ASSUME 10' CUBE MODULE:

40'

30'

ROOF PLAN

20'

ELEVATION   ELEVATION

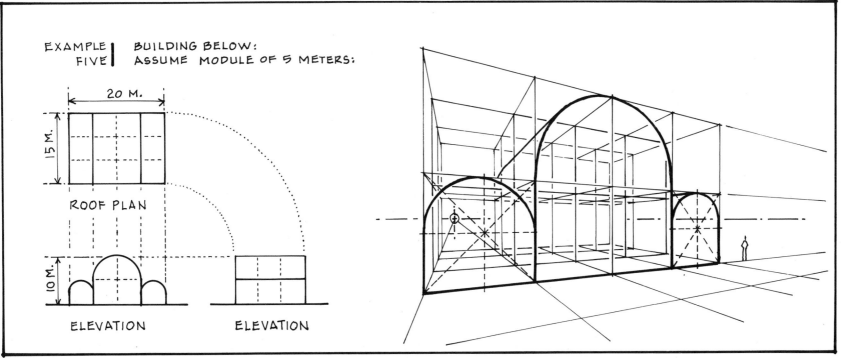

EXAMPLE FIVE | BUILDING BELOW:
ASSUME MODULE OF 5 METERS:

20 M.

15 M.

ROOF PLAN

10 M.

ELEVATION   ELEVATION

EXERCISE #3

CUBE - MODULE PERSPECTIVE: 2 - POINT

CUT AWAY THE NEXT SHEET AT DASHED LINE ⟶
TAPE THE SHEET TO YOUR DRAWING BOARD.

FIRST, DIVIDE
THE CUBE INTO
8 EQUAL
CUBES.
THEN, EXPAND
BY LIKE CUBES
TO THE FORM
INDICATED
IN ONE OF
THESE VARIATIONS
(A, B, C, or D)
AS ASSIGNED
BY YOUR
INSTRUCTOR.

THIS IS A
TRANSPARENT
FRAME:
ALL LINES ARE
TO BE SEEN
IN THE
PERSPECTIVE
(UNLESS HIDDEN
BY OTHER LINES).

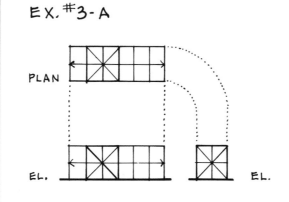

EX. #3-A

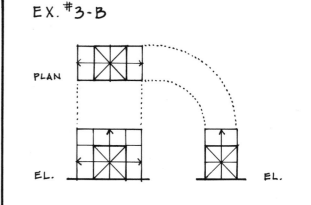

EX. #3-B

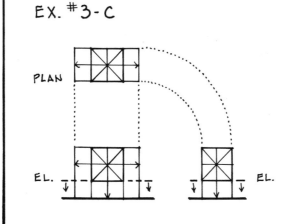

EX. #3-C

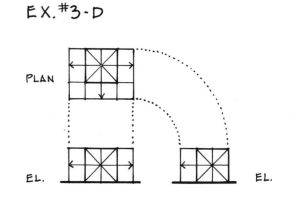

EX. #3-D

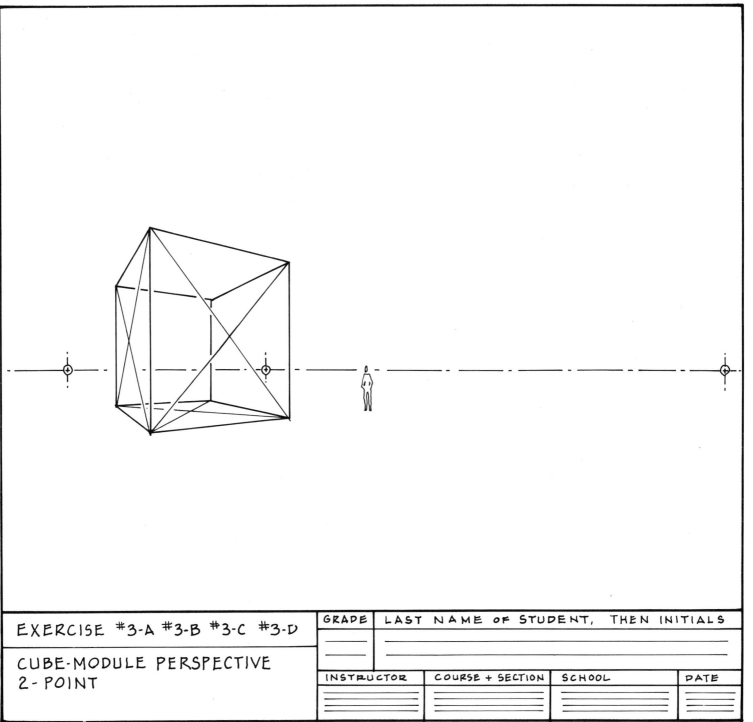

EXERCISE #3-A #3-B #3-C #3-D	GRADE	LAST NAME OF STUDENT, THEN INITIALS			
CUBE-MODULE PERSPECTIVE 2-POINT		INSTRUCTOR	COURSE + SECTION	SCHOOL	DATE

(DO NOT REMOVE THIS SHEET: NEW STUDY ON OTHER SIDE.)

CUBE-MODULE PERSPECTIVE: 2-POINT

TRACE LIGHTLY YOUR CUBE-MODULE FRAME OF EX.#3. ON THAT "PENCIL SCAFFOLDING"
DRAW CLEARLY THE RELATED BUILDING FORM FROM BELOW (A, B, C OR D).

EX. #4-A

ROOF PLAN

FRONT EL.

END EL.

EX. #4-B

ROOF PLAN

FRONT EL.

END EL.

ALSO ON YOUR TRACING SHEET, COMPLETE THE TITLE BOX WITH ADJUSTED INFORMATION.

EX. #4-C

ROOF PLAN

FRONT EL.

END EL.

EX. #4-D

ROOF PLAN

FRONT EL.

END EL.

EYE JUDGMENT OF CUBES IN 3-POINT PERSPECTIVE

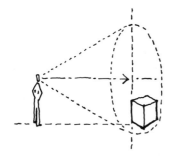

← STILL 2-POINT PERSPECTIVE

OBJECT (CUBE) IS IN LOWER PART OF OBSERVER'S CONE OF VISION WITH ITS HORIZONTAL LINE OF SIGHT.

THE PICTURE PLANE REMAINS VERTICAL.

VERTICAL LINES REMAIN VERTICAL.

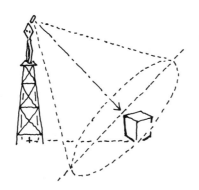

← 3-POINT PERSPECTIVE

PICTURE PLANE, LINE OF SIGHT AND CONE OF VISION ALL TILT.

CUBE'S VERTICAL LINES NOW HAVE A VANISHING POINT. (THE THIRD VAN. PT. FOR A RECTANGULAR OBJECT)

CUBE JUDGMENT NOW REQUIRES ANOTHER CONSIDERATION, AS ALL 3 VISIBLE PLANES ARE FORE-SHORTENED WITHOUT PARALLELS REMAINING.

2-POINT PERSPECTIVE

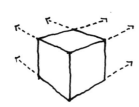

3-POINT PERSPECTIVES

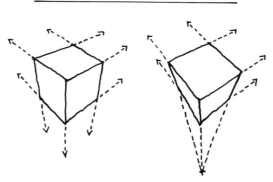

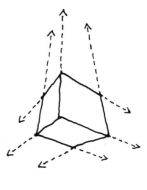

3-POINT PERSPECTIVE IS MECHANICALLY CONSTRUCTABLE FROM PLAN AND ELEVATION, BUT IT IS A LABORIOUS PROCESS, AND THE MECHANICS DO NOT NECESSARILY PRODUCE VISUAL SATISFACTION. WE SHOW HERE OUR CUBE-JUDGMENT SYSTEM FOR 3-POINT PERSPECTIVE.

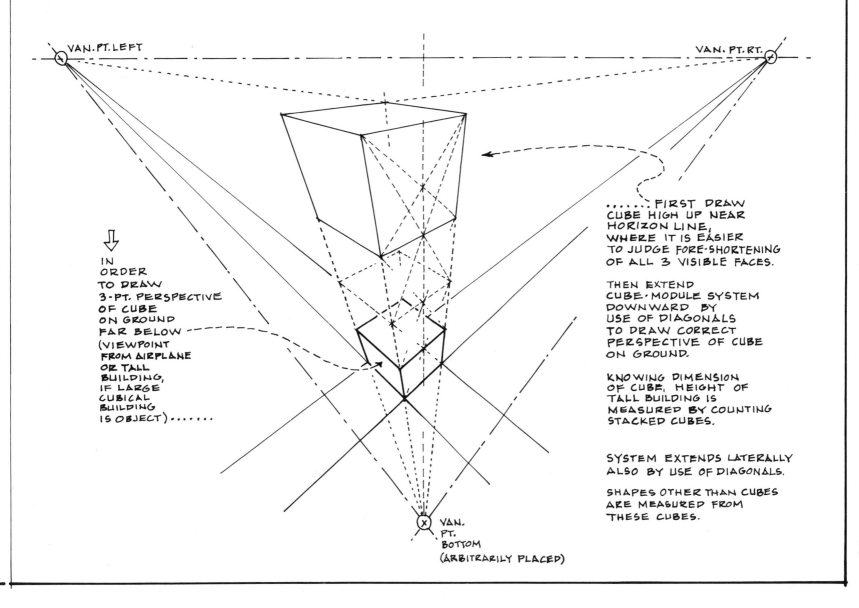

VAN. PT. LEFT

VAN. PT. RT.

IN ORDER TO DRAW 3-PT. PERSPECTIVE OF CUBE ON GROUND FAR BELOW — (VIEWPOINT FROM AIRPLANE OR TALL BUILDING, IF LARGE CUBICAL BUILDING IS OBJECT) ....

......FIRST DRAW CUBE HIGH UP NEAR HORIZON LINE, WHERE IT IS EASIER TO JUDGE FORE-SHORTENING OF ALL 3 VISIBLE FACES.

THEN EXTEND CUBE-MODULE SYSTEM DOWNWARD BY USE OF DIAGONALS TO DRAW CORRECT PERSPECTIVE OF CUBE ON GROUND.

KNOWING DIMENSION OF CUBE, HEIGHT OF TALL BUILDING IS MEASURED BY COUNTING STACKED CUBES.

SYSTEM EXTENDS LATERALLY ALSO BY USE OF DIAGONALS.

SHAPES OTHER THAN CUBES ARE MEASURED FROM THESE CUBES.

VAN. PT. BOTTOM (ARBITRARILY PLACED)

EXERCISE #5

CUBE-MODULE PERSPECTIVE: 3-POINT

CUT AWAY THE NEXT SHEET AT DASHED LINE ————————————>
TAPE THE SHEET TO YOUR DRAWING BOARD.

EXTEND THE
ESTIMATED CUBE
DOWNWARD BY
4 MORE CUBES.
ASSUME THAT
THE BOTTOM CUBE
OF THE 5 CUBES
SITS ON THE
FLAT GROUND.
NOW EXPAND
THAT BOTTOM
CUBE TO THE
CLUSTER SHOWN
IN ONE OF
THESE VARIATIONS
(A, B, C, OR D)
AS ASSIGNED BY
YOUR INSTRUCTOR.

THIS IS A
TRANSPARENT
FRAME:
SHOW ALL ITS
LINES IN YOUR
PERSPECTIVE.

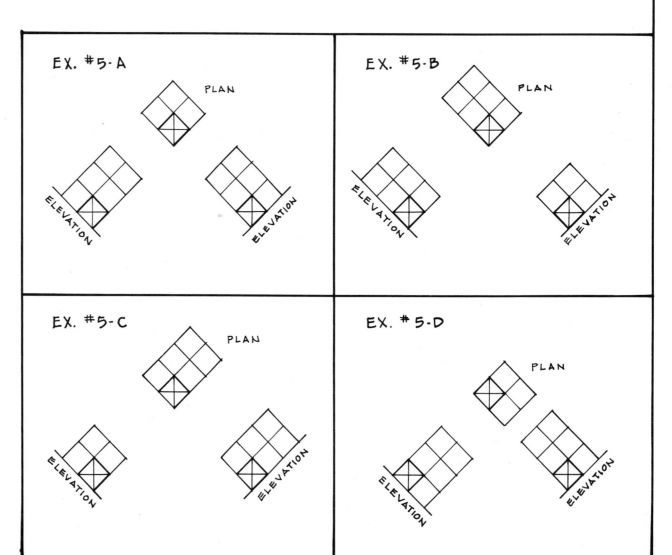

EX. #5-A

EX. #5-B

EX. #5-C

EX. #5-D

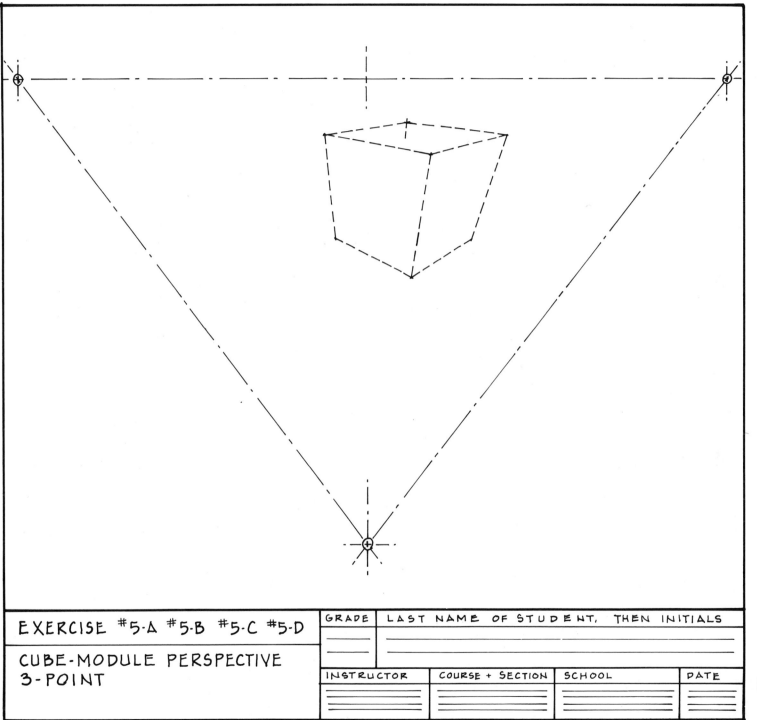

EXERCISE #5·A #5·B #5·C #5·D

CUBE·MODULE PERSPECTIVE
3·POINT

GRADE	LAST NAME OF STUDENT, THEN INITIALS

INSTRUCTOR	COURSE + SECTION	SCHOOL	DATE

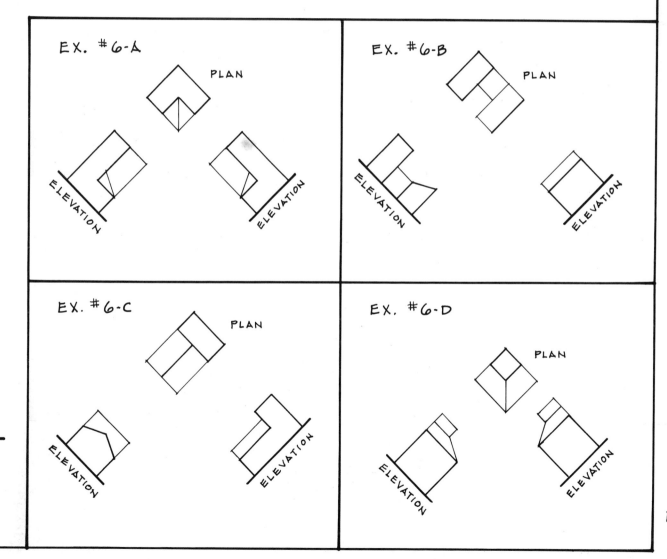

EXERCISE #6   (DO NOT REMOVE THIS SHEET: NEW STUDY ON OTHER SIDE.)

CUBE-MODULE PERSPECTIVE: 3-POINT

TRACE LIGHTLY YOUR CUBE-MODULE FRAME OF EX. #5. ON THAT "PENCIL SCAFFOLDING" DRAW CLEARLY THE RELATED BUILDING FORM FROM BELOW (A, B, C OR D).

ALSO ON YOUR TRACING SHEET, COMPLETE THE TITLE BOX WITH ADJUSTED INFORMATION.

EX. #6-A   PLAN   ELEVATION   ELEVATION

EX. #6-B   PLAN   ELEVATION   ELEVATION

EX. #6-C   PLAN   ELEVATION   ELEVATION

EX. #6-D   PLAN   ELEVATION   ELEVATION

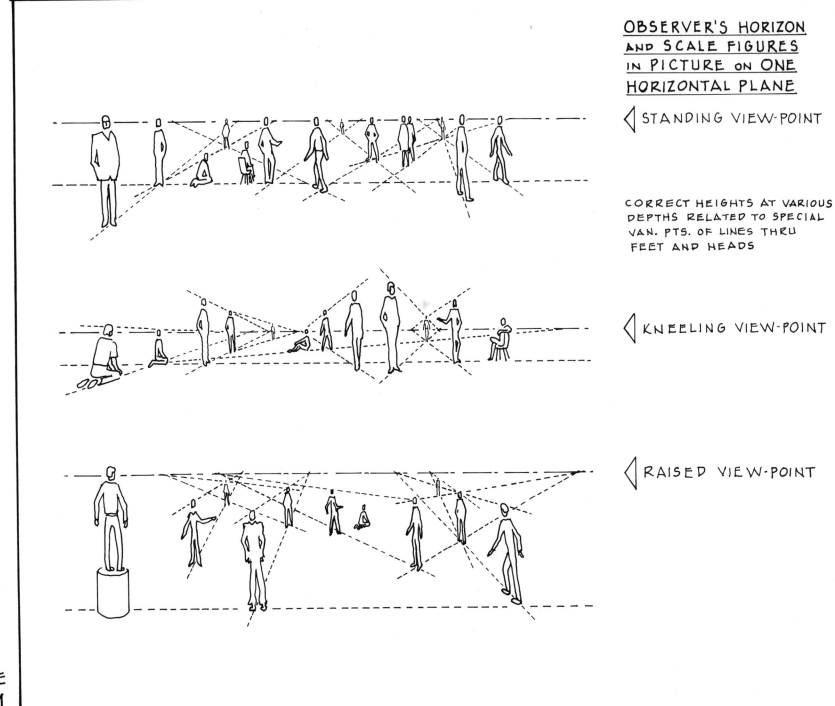

OBSERVER'S HORIZON
AND SCALE FIGURES
IN PICTURE ON ONE
HORIZONTAL PLANE

◁ STANDING VIEW-POINT

CORRECT HEIGHTS AT VARIOUS
DEPTHS RELATED TO SPECIAL
VAN. PTS. OF LINES THRU
FEET AND HEADS

◁ KNEELING VIEW-POINT

◁ RAISED VIEW-POINT

STUDY No 8

PAGE
34

GEOMETRIC SCALE FIGURES

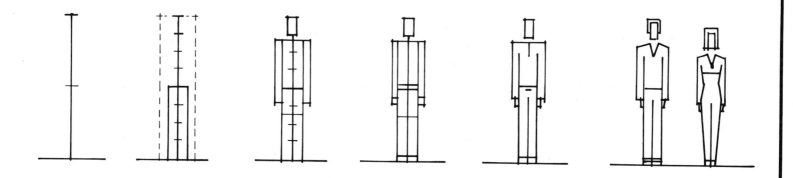

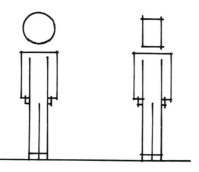

HEAD
WRONG SHAPE
OR TOO LARGE
OR TOO SMALL
THROWS
PICTURE
OUT OF SCALE

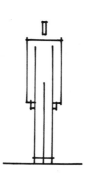

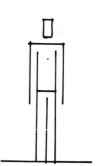

HEAD AS
VERTICAL
RECTANGLE
ABOUT 1/8
TO 1/7
HEIGHT OF
FIGURE

NOTE: EXAGGERATED, DISTORTED OR
CARTOON SCALE FIGURES MAY DISTURB
THE CLIENT.

FIGURES REQUIRE HUMAN PROPORTIONS
TO ENHANCE THE ILLUSTRATION
RATHER THAN DISTRACT.

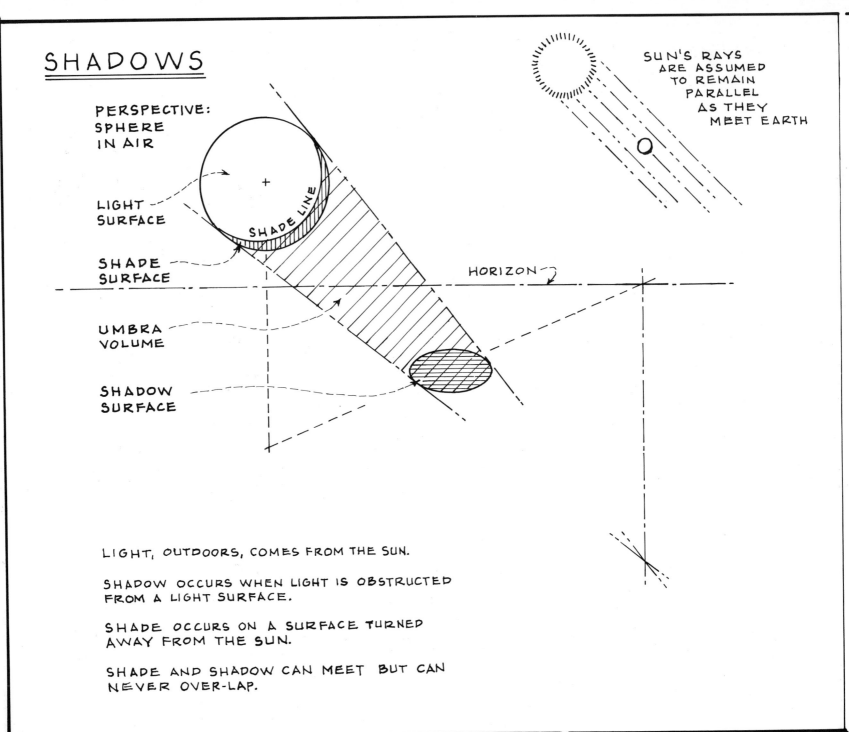

SHADOWS

PERSPECTIVE:
SPHERE
IN AIR

SUN'S RAYS
ARE ASSUMED
TO REMAIN
PARALLEL
AS THEY
MEET EARTH

SHADE LINE

LIGHT
SURFACE

SHADE
SURFACE

HORIZON

UMBRA
VOLUME

SHADOW
SURFACE

LIGHT, OUTDOORS, COMES FROM THE SUN.

SHADOW OCCURS WHEN LIGHT IS OBSTRUCTED
FROM A LIGHT SURFACE.

SHADE OCCURS ON A SURFACE TURNED
AWAY FROM THE SUN.

SHADE AND SHADOW CAN MEET BUT CAN
NEVER OVER-LAP.

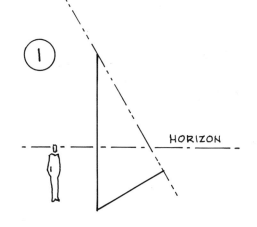

(1) CHOOSE SHADOW OF POLE
ON GROUND   (= SHADOW
OF VERTICAL LINE ON
HORIZONTAL PLANE).

HORIZON

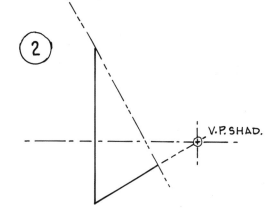

(2) EXTEND SHADOW TO FIND
ITS VANISHING POINT ON
HORIZON LINE. (SHADOWS
OF ALL VERT. LINES ON
HORIZ. PLANES VANISH HERE.)

V.P.SHAD.

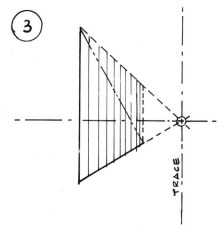

(3) EXTEND VERT. PLANE
OF POLE, SHADOW AND
SUN-RAY TO MEET
PICTURE PLANE ON
VERT. LINE CALLED "TRACE".

TRACE

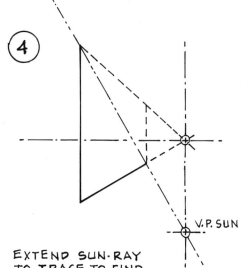

(4) EXTEND SUN-RAY
TO TRACE TO FIND
VANISHING POINT
FOR ALL SUN-RAYS.

V.P. SUN

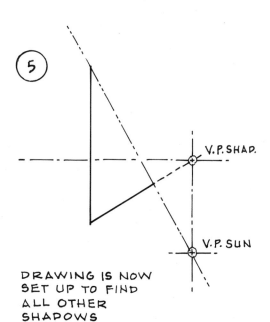

(5) DRAWING IS NOW
SET UP TO FIND
ALL OTHER
SHADOWS

V.P.SHAD.

V.P. SUN

(6) ADD SHADOW OF
SCALE FIGURE
(WHICH IS BASICALLY
ANOTHER POLE).

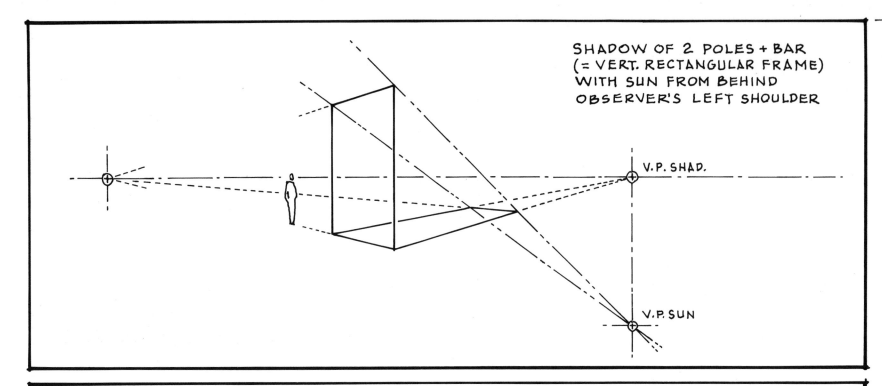

SHADOW OF 2 POLES + BAR
(= VERT. RECTANGULAR FRAME)
WITH SUN FROM BEHIND
OBSERVER'S LEFT SHOULDER

V.P. SHAD.

V.P. SUN

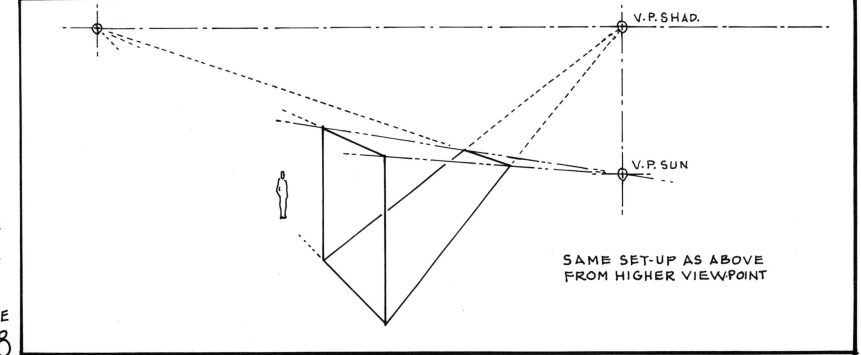

V.P. SHAD.

V.P. SUN

SAME SET-UP AS ABOVE
FROM HIGHER VIEWPOINT

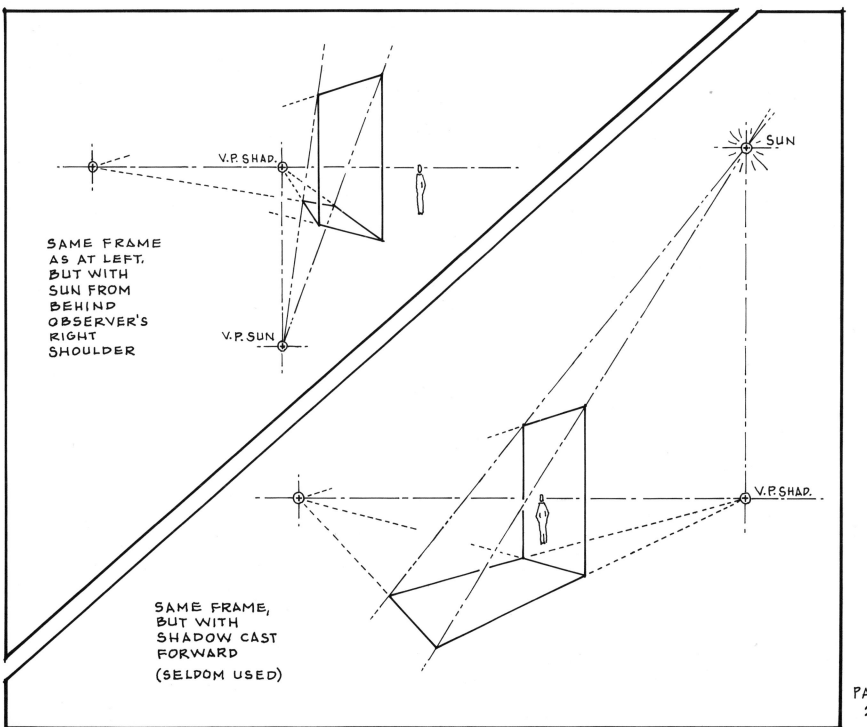

SAME FRAME
AS AT LEFT,
BUT WITH
SUN FROM
BEHIND
OBSERVER'S
RIGHT
SHOULDER

V.P. SHAD.

V.P. SUN

SUN

V.P. SHAD.

SAME FRAME,
BUT WITH
SHADOW CAST
FORWARD
(SELDOM USED)

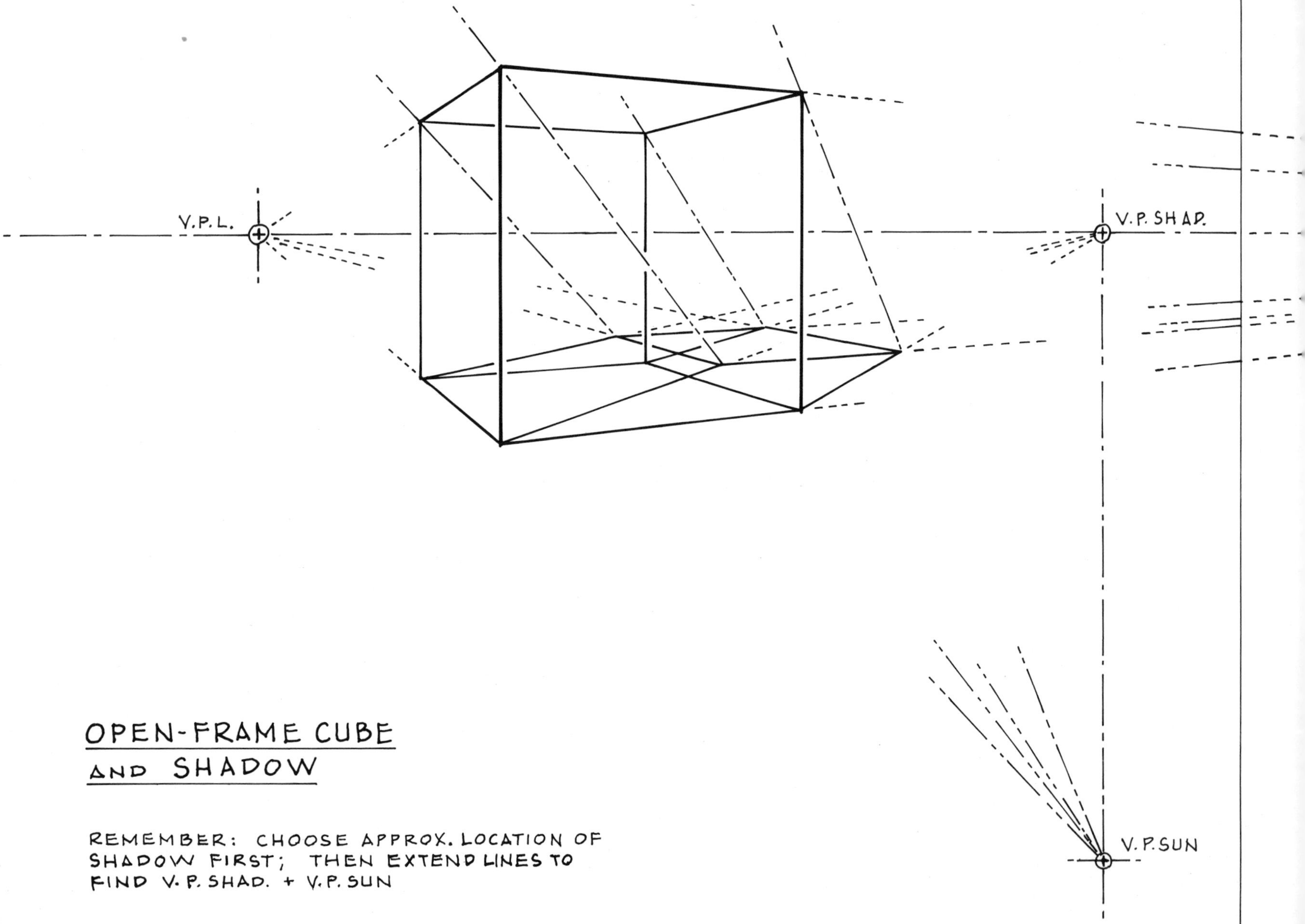

V.P.L.

V.P. SHAD.

V.P. SUN

OPEN-FRAME CUBE
AND SHADOW

REMEMBER: CHOOSE APPROX. LOCATION OF
SHADOW FIRST; THEN EXTEND LINES TO
FIND V.P. SHAD. + V.P. SUN

V.P.R.

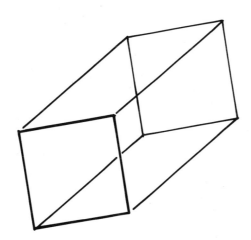

<u>PLAN</u>
WITH SHADOW

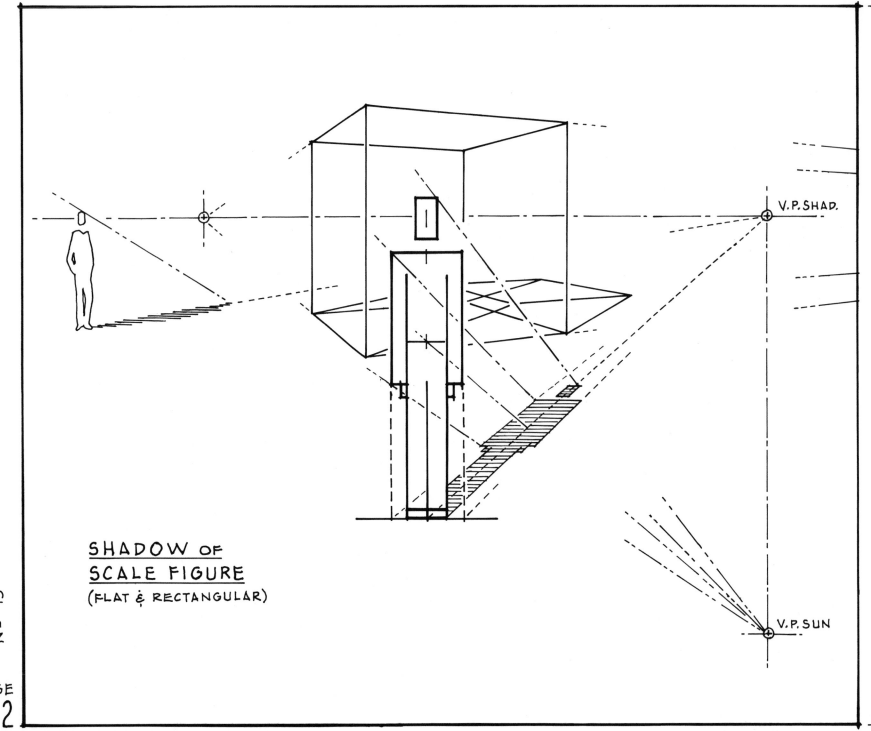

SHADOW OF
SCALE FIGURE
(FLAT & RECTANGULAR)

V.P.SHAD.

V.P.SUN

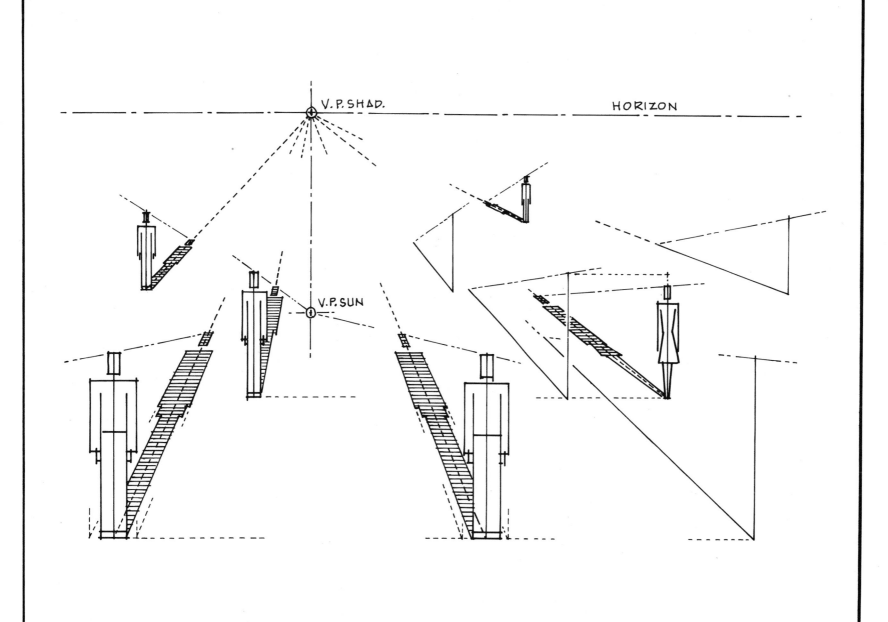

V.P.SHAD.   HORIZON

V.P.SUN

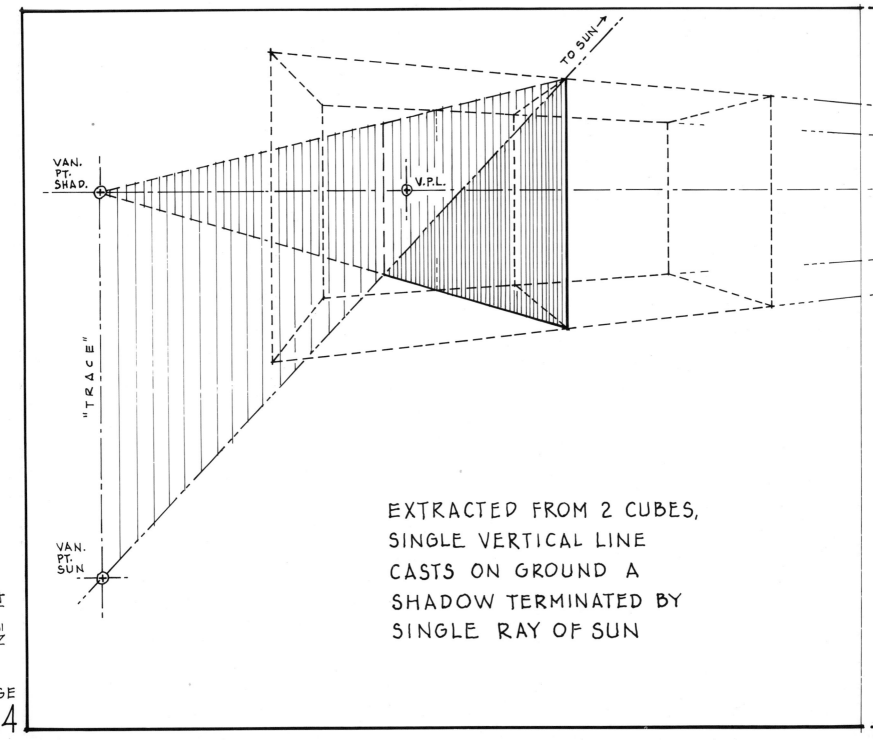

VAN.
PT.
SHAD.

V.P.L.

TO SUN

"TRACE"

VAN.
PT.
SUN

EXTRACTED FROM 2 CUBES,
SINGLE VERTICAL LINE
CASTS ON GROUND A
SHADOW TERMINATED BY
SINGLE RAY OF SUN

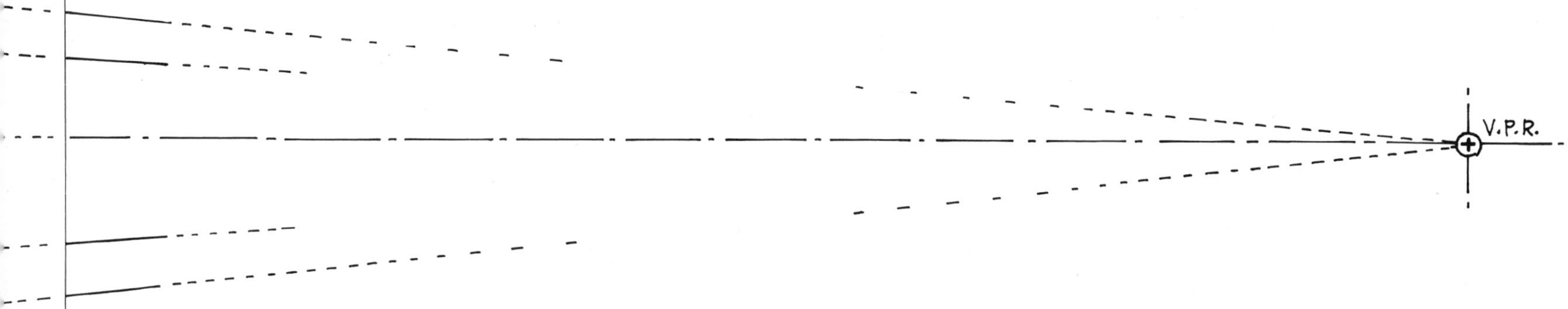

V.P.R.

NOTE RELATION TO CUBE OF VERTICAL PLANE
CONTAINING SUN-RAY, VERTICAL LINE AND SHADOW.
OBSERVE HOW THIS PLANE CUTS CEILING IN A
HORIZONTAL LINE WHICH AIMS AT VAN. PT. SHAD.:
THIS WILL BE USEFUL.

THIS VERTICAL PLANE
MEETS PICTURE PLANE
IN VERTICAL LINE (= "TRACE")
WHICH CONTAINS BOTH
VAN. PT. SHADOWS AND
VAN. PT. SUN RAYS.

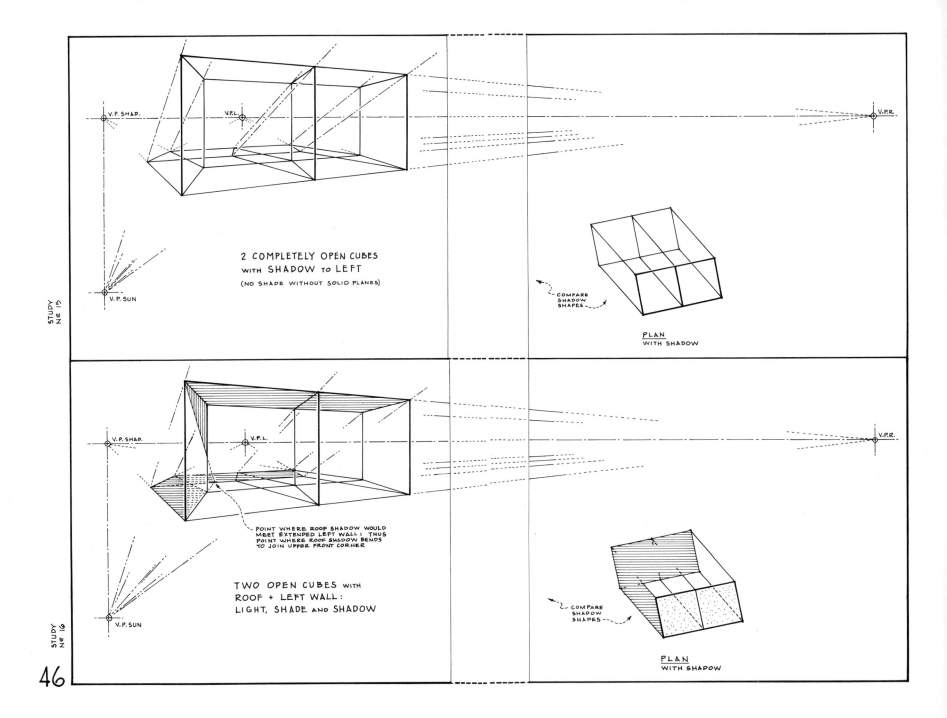

V. P. SHAD.

V.P.L.

V.P.R.

V. P. SUN

2 COMPLETELY OPEN CUBES
WITH SHADOW TO LEFT

(NO SHADE WITHOUT SOLID PLANES)

COMPARE
SHADOW
SHAPES

PLAN
WITH SHADOW

V. P. SHAD.

V.P.L.

V.P.R.

POINT WHERE ROOF SHADOW WOULD
MEET EXTENDED LEFT WALL: THUS
POINT WHERE ROOF SHADOW BENDS
TO JOIN UPPER FRONT CORNER

V. P. SUN

TWO OPEN CUBES WITH
ROOF + LEFT WALL:
LIGHT, SHADE AND SHADOW

COMPARE
SHADOW
SHAPES

PLAN
WITH SHADOW

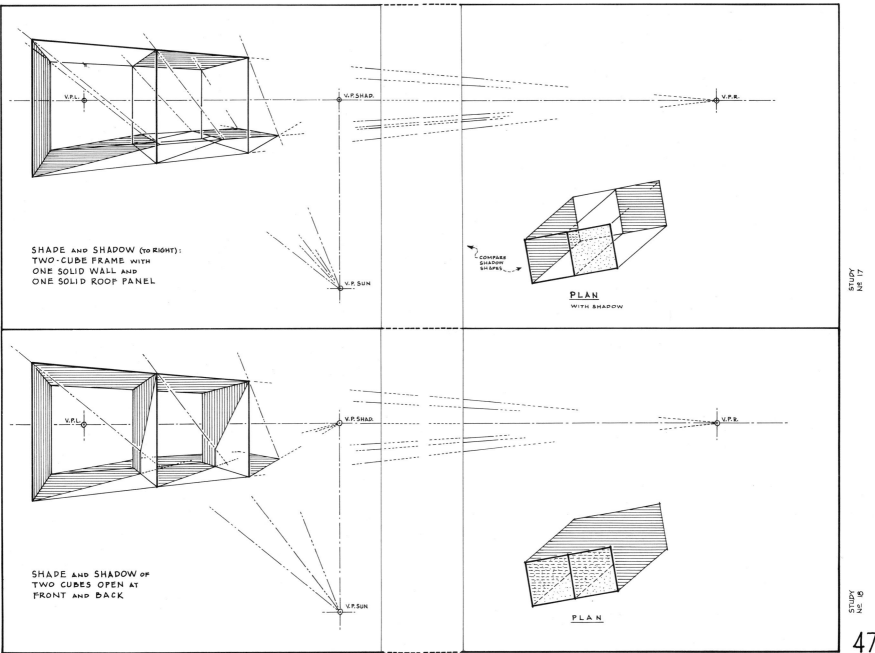

SHADE and SHADOW (TO RIGHT):
TWO-CUBE FRAME with
ONE SOLID WALL and
ONE SOLID ROOF PANEL

V.P.L.

V.P. SHAD.

V.P.R.

V.P. SUN

COMPARE
SHADOW
SHAPES

PLAN
WITH SHADOW

SHADE and SHADOW of
TWO CUBES OPEN at
FRONT and BACK

V.P.L.

V.P. SHAD.

V.P.R.

V.P. SUN

PLAN

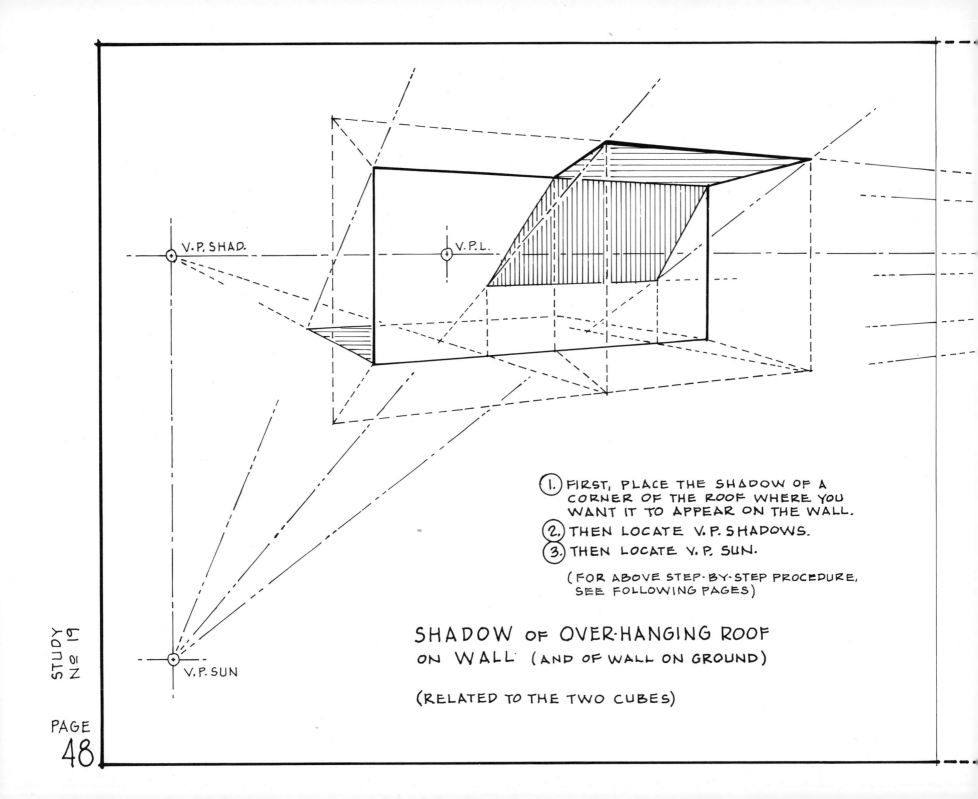

V.P. SHAD.

V.P.L.

1. FIRST, PLACE THE SHADOW OF A CORNER OF THE ROOF WHERE YOU WANT IT TO APPEAR ON THE WALL.
2. THEN LOCATE V.P. SHADOWS.
3. THEN LOCATE V.P. SUN.

(FOR ABOVE STEP·BY·STEP PROCEDURE, SEE FOLLOWING PAGES)

V.P. SUN

SHADOW OF OVER·HANGING ROOF ON WALL (AND OF WALL ON GROUND)

(RELATED TO THE TWO CUBES)

STUDY № 19

PAGE 48

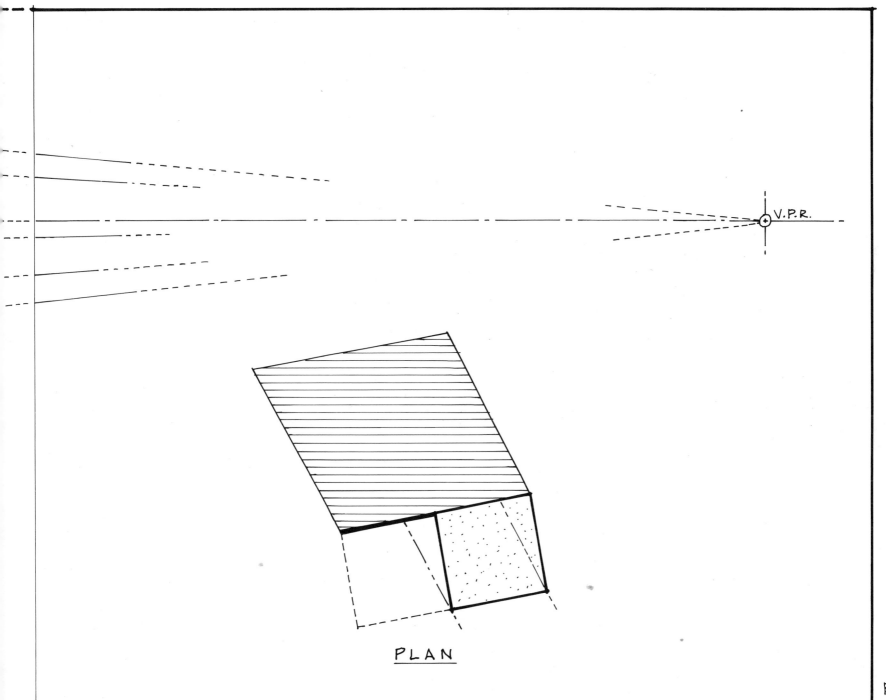

V.P.R.

PLAN

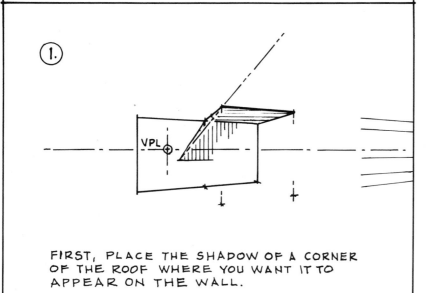

① FIRST, PLACE THE SHADOW OF A CORNER OF THE ROOF WHERE YOU WANT IT TO APPEAR ON THE WALL.

THIS GIVES YOU CONTROL OF THE PRINCIPAL SHADOW, PLUS THE MEANS TO LOCATE V.P. SHAD. AND V.P. SUN.

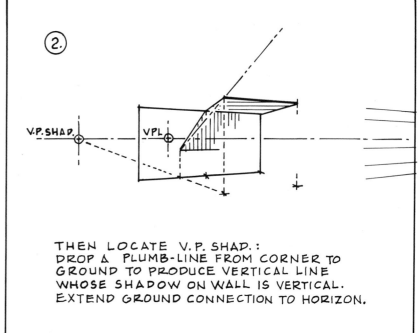

② THEN LOCATE V.P. SHAD.: DROP A PLUMB-LINE FROM CORNER TO GROUND TO PRODUCE VERTICAL LINE WHOSE SHADOW ON WALL IS VERTICAL. EXTEND GROUND CONNECTION TO HORIZON.

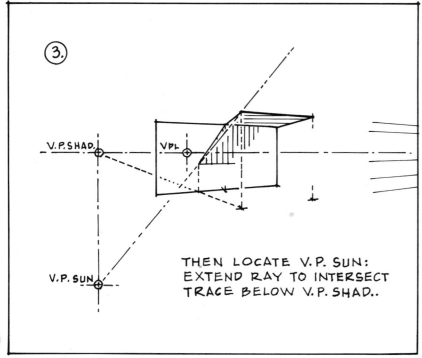

③ THEN LOCATE V.P. SUN: EXTEND RAY TO INTERSECT TRACE BELOW V.P. SHAD..

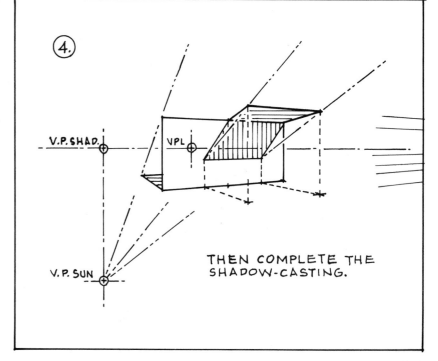

④ THEN COMPLETE THE SHADOW-CASTING.

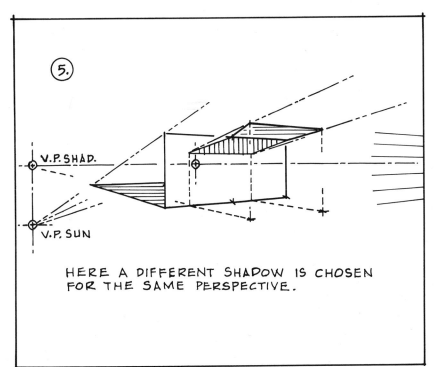

⑤

V.P. SHAD.

V.P. SUN

HERE A DIFFERENT SHADOW IS CHOSEN
FOR THE SAME PERSPECTIVE.

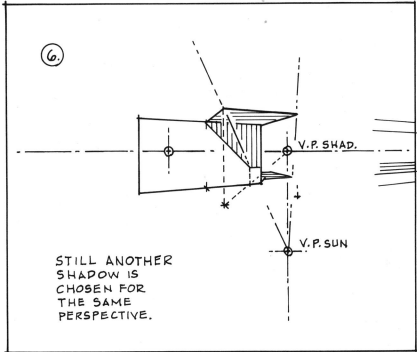

⑥

V.P. SHAD.

V.P. SUN

STILL ANOTHER
SHADOW IS
CHOSEN FOR
THE SAME
PERSPECTIVE.

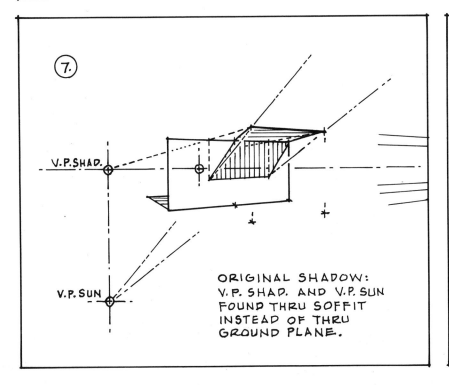

⑦

V.P. SHAD.

V.P. SUN

ORIGINAL SHADOW:
V.P. SHAD. AND V.P. SUN
FOUND THRU SOFFIT
INSTEAD OF THRU
GROUND PLANE.

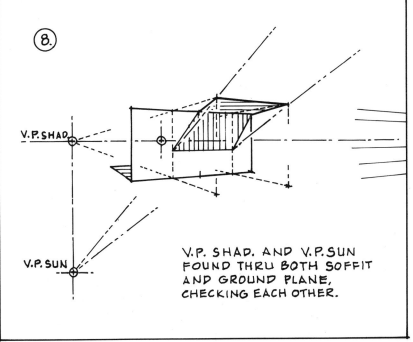

⑧

V.P. SHAD.

V.P. SUN

V.P. SHAD. AND V.P. SUN
FOUND THRU BOTH SOFFIT
AND GROUND PLANE,
CHECKING EACH OTHER.

PAGE
51

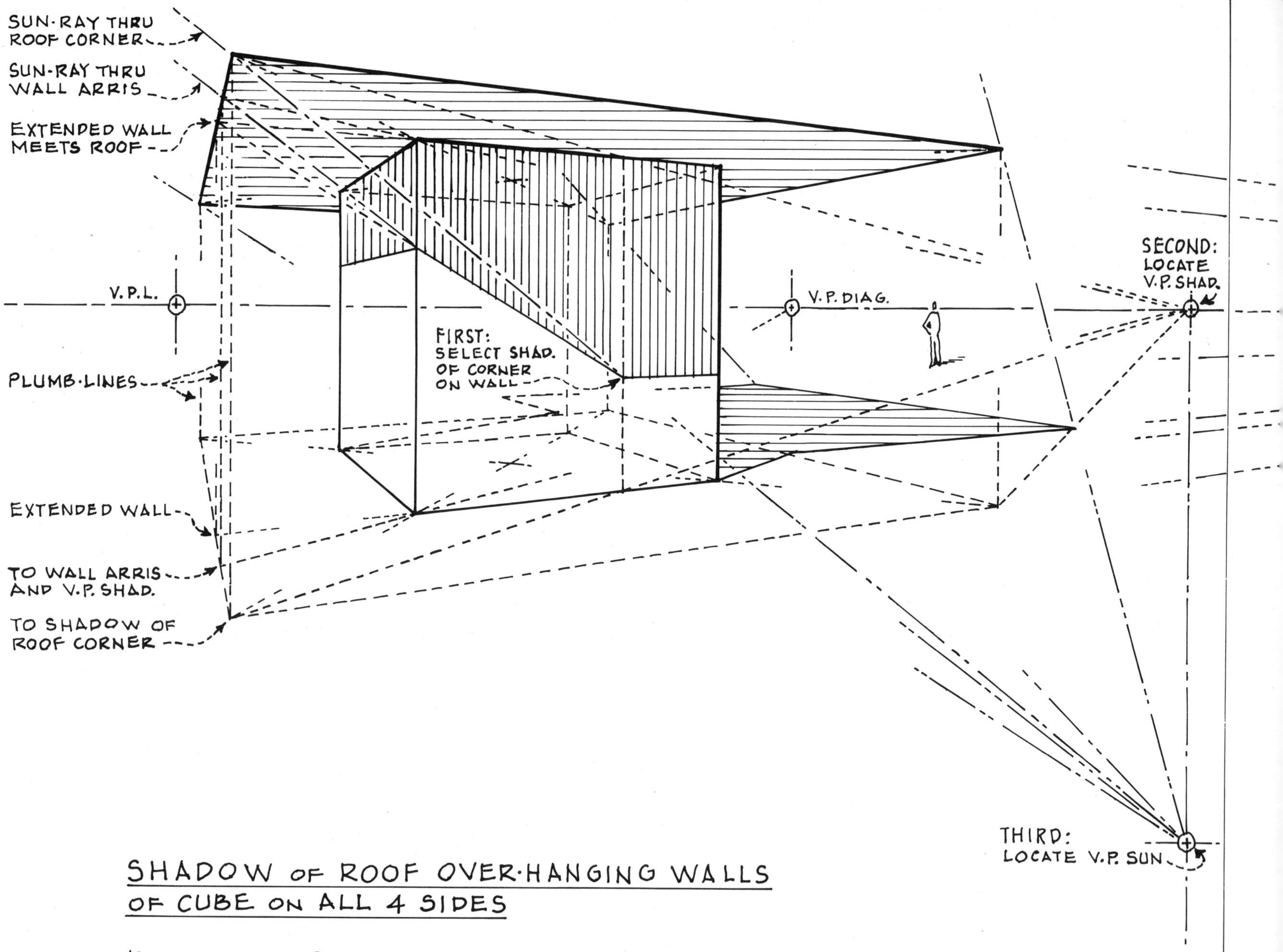

SUN·RAY THRU
ROOF CORNER

SUN·RAY THRU
WALL ARRIS

EXTENDED WALL
MEETS ROOF

V.P.L.

PLUMB·LINES

EXTENDED WALL

TO WALL ARRIS
AND V.P. SHAD.

TO SHADOW OF
ROOF CORNER

FIRST:
SELECT SHAD.
OF CORNER
ON WALL

V.P. DIAG.

SECOND:
LOCATE
V.P. SHAD.

THIRD:
LOCATE V.P. SUN.

SHADOW OF ROOF OVER·HANGING WALLS
OF CUBE ON ALL 4 SIDES

FOUND THRU GROUND, THRU SOFFIT, AND THRU
EXTENDED WALL: THE 3 METHODS CHECK
EACH OTHER. (SEE FOLLOWING DRAWINGS.)

STUDY
Nᵒ 20

PAGE
52

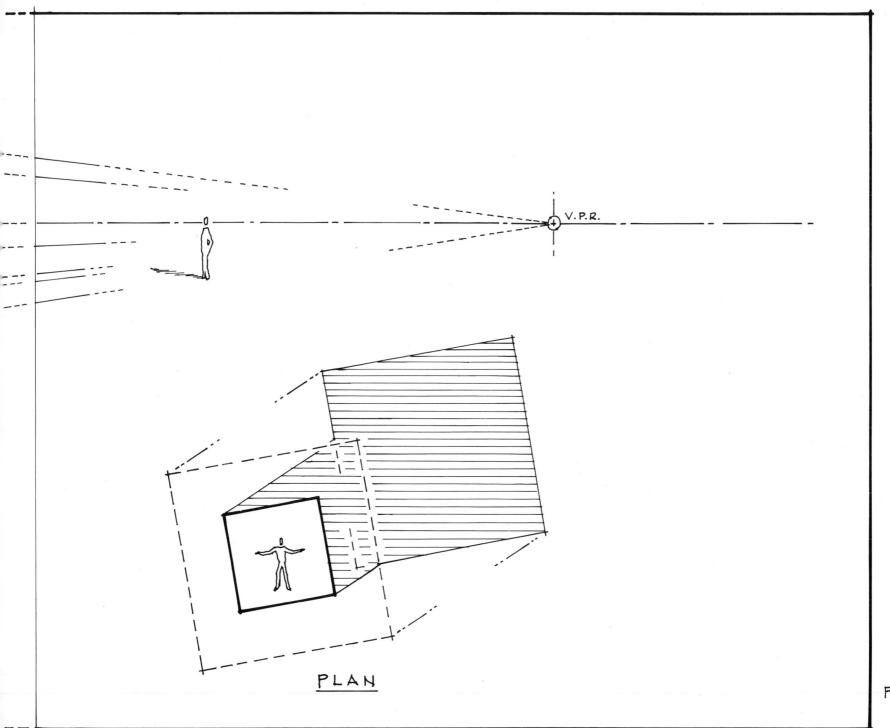

V.P.R.

PLAN

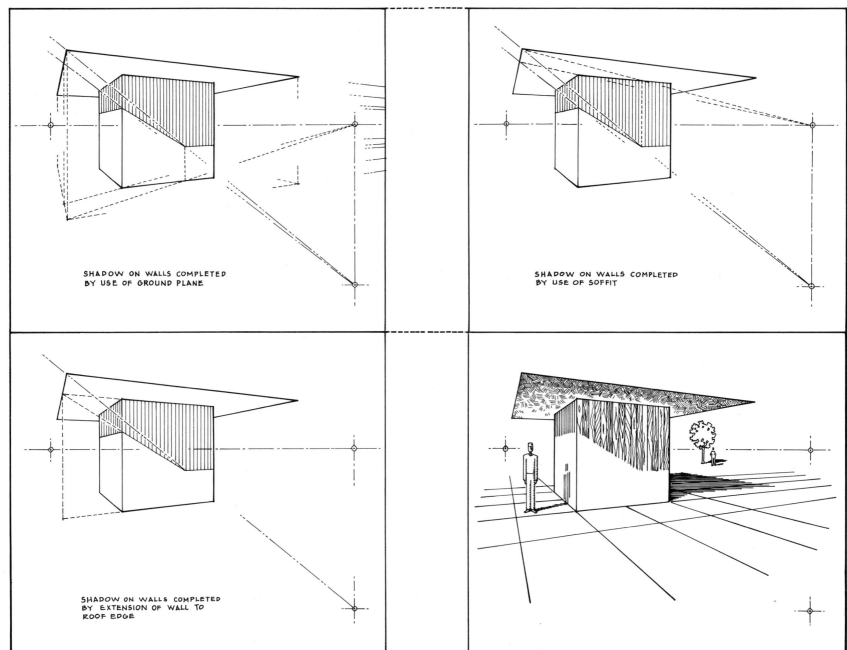

SHADOW ON WALLS COMPLETED
BY USE OF GROUND PLANE

SHADOW ON WALLS COMPLETED
BY USE OF SOFFIT

SHADOW ON WALLS COMPLETED
BY EXTENSION OF WALL TO
ROOF EDGE

54

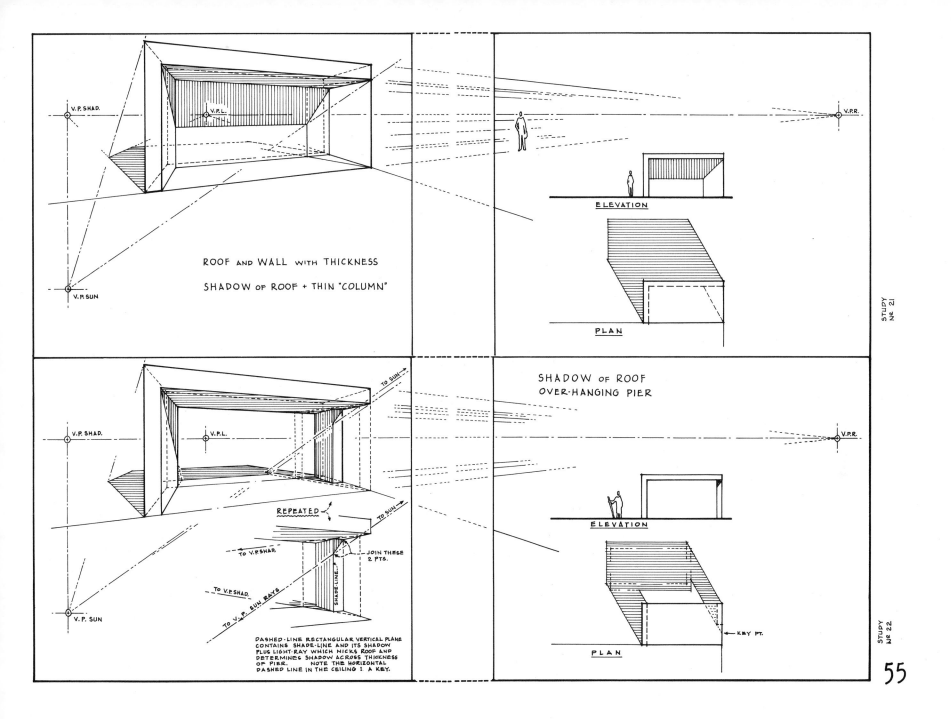

ROOF and WALL with THICKNESS

SHADOW of ROOF + THIN "COLUMN"

V.P. SHAD.

V.P.L.

V.P.SUN

V.P.R.

ELEVATION

PLAN

SHADOW of ROOF
OVER-HANGING PIER

V.P. SHAD.

V.P.L.

V.P.SUN

V.P.R.

REPEATED

TO SUN

TO SUN

TO V.P. SHAD.

JOIN THESE 2 PTS.

SHADE-LINE

TO V.P. SHAD.

TO V.P. SUN RAYS

DASHED-LINE RECTANGULAR VERTICAL PLANE
CONTAINS SHADE-LINE AND ITS SHADOW
PLUS LIGHT-RAY WHICH NICKS ROOF AND
DETERMINES SHADOW ACROSS THICKNESS
OF PIER.   NOTE THE HORIZONTAL
DASHED LINE IN THE CEILING : A KEY.

ELEVATION

PLAN

KEY PT.

55

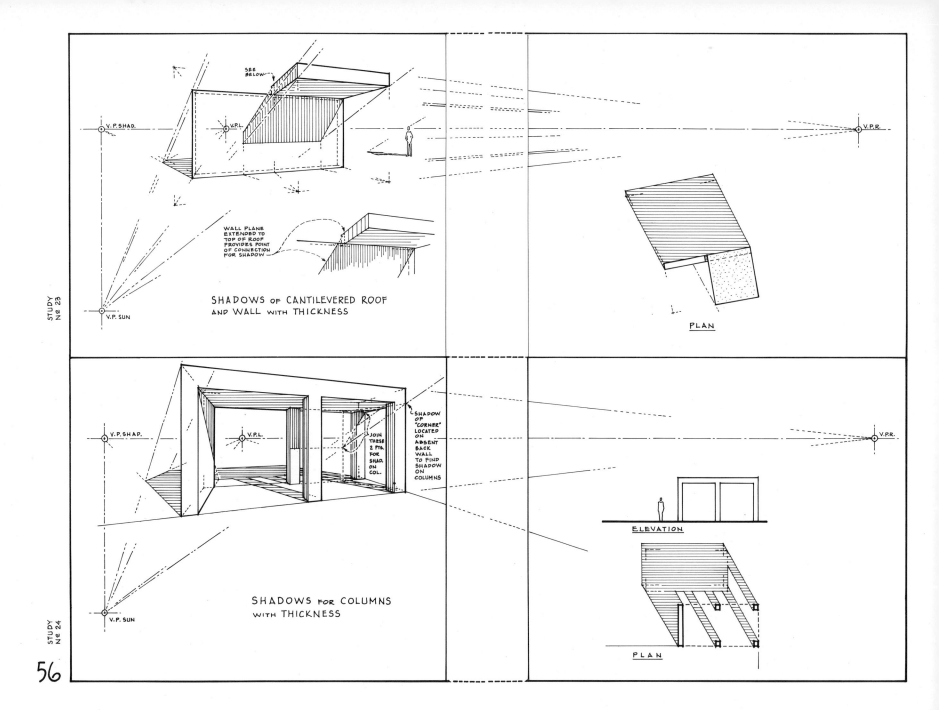

SEE
BELOW

V.P.SHAD.

V.P.L.

V.P.R.

WALL PLANE
EXTENDED TO
TOP OF ROOF
PROVIDES POINT
OF CONNECTION
FOR SHADOW

V.P. SUN

SHADOWS of CANTILEVERED ROOF
AND WALL with THICKNESS

PLAN

V.P.SHAD.

V.P.L.

V.P.R.

JOIN
THESE
2 PTS.
FOR
SHAD.
ON
COL.

SHADOW
OF
"CORNER"
LOCATED
ON
ABSENT
BACK
WALL
TO FIND
SHADOW
ON
COLUMNS

V.P. SUN

SHADOWS FOR COLUMNS
with THICKNESS

ELEVATION

PLAN

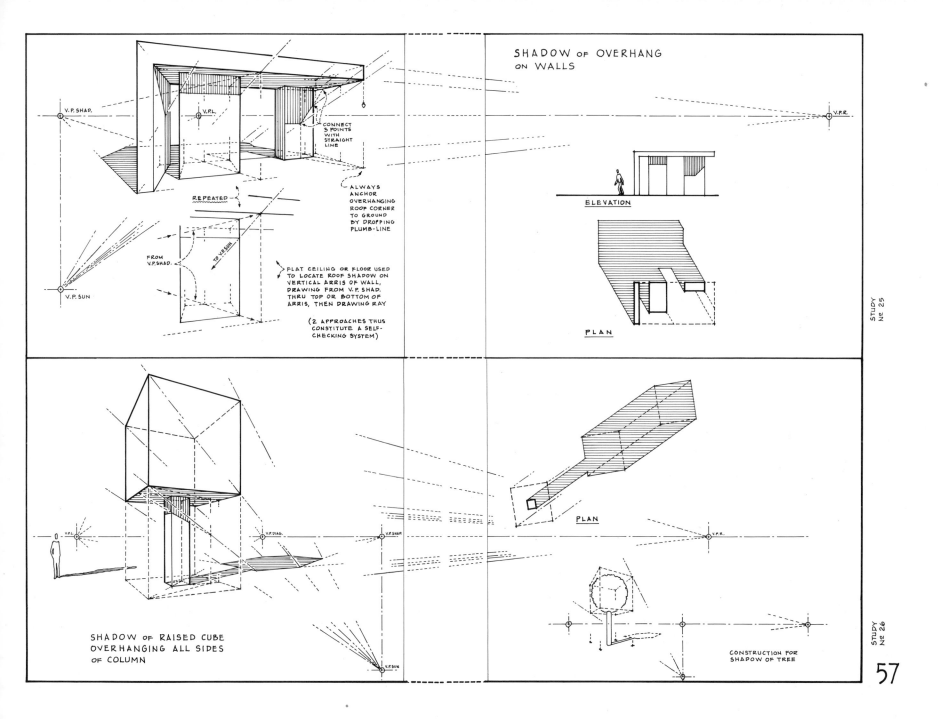

SHADOW of OVERHANG
on WALLS

V.P.SHAD.

V.P.L.

V.P.R.

CONNECT
3 POINTS
WITH
STRAIGHT
LINE

ALWAYS
ANCHOR
OVERHANGING
ROOF CORNER
TO GROUND
BY DROPPING
PLUMB-LINE

REPEATED

FROM
V.P.SHAD.

TO V.P.SUN

V.P. SUN

FLAT CEILING OR FLOOR USED
TO LOCATE ROOF SHADOW ON
VERTICAL ARRIS OF WALL,
DRAWING FROM V.P. SHAD.
THRU TOP OR BOTTOM OF
ARRIS, THEN DRAWING RAY

(2 APPROACHES THUS
CONSTITUTE A SELF-
CHECKING SYSTEM)

ELEVATION

PLAN

V.P.L.

V.F. DIAG.

V.F.SHAD.

V.P.R.

PLAN

SHADOW of RAISED CUBE
OVERHANGING ALL SIDES
of COLUMN

V.P.SUN

CONSTRUCTION FOR
SHADOW OF TREE

STANDING OBSERVER PLUS PEOPLE OF
SAME HEIGHT AND TREES OF ONE HEIGHT,
ALL ON SINGLE HORIZONTAL PLANE

V. P.
SHAD.

V. P.
SUN

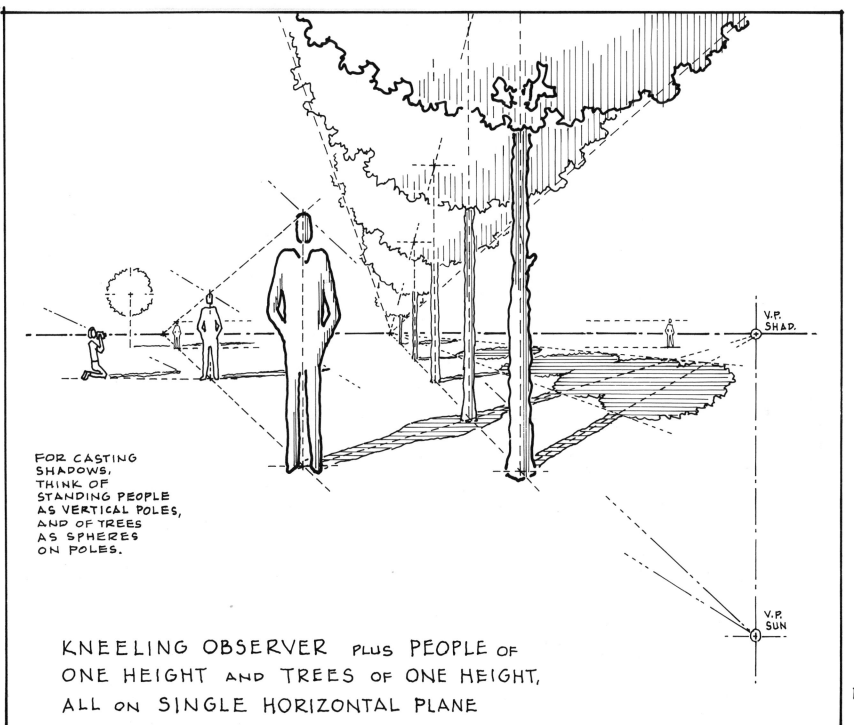

FOR CASTING
SHADOWS,
THINK OF
STANDING PEOPLE
AS VERTICAL POLES,
AND OF TREES
AS SPHERES
ON POLES.

V.P.
SHAD.

V.P.
SUN

KNEELING OBSERVER PLUS PEOPLE OF
ONE HEIGHT AND TREES OF ONE HEIGHT,
ALL ON SINGLE HORIZONTAL PLANE

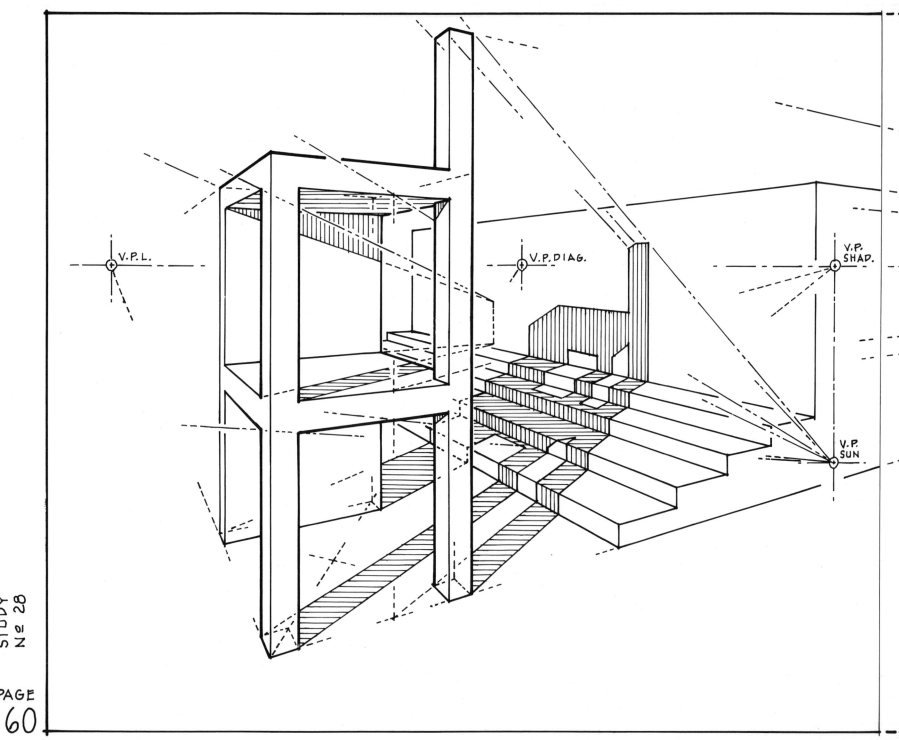

V.P.L.

V.P. DIAG.

V.P. SHAD.

V.P. SUN

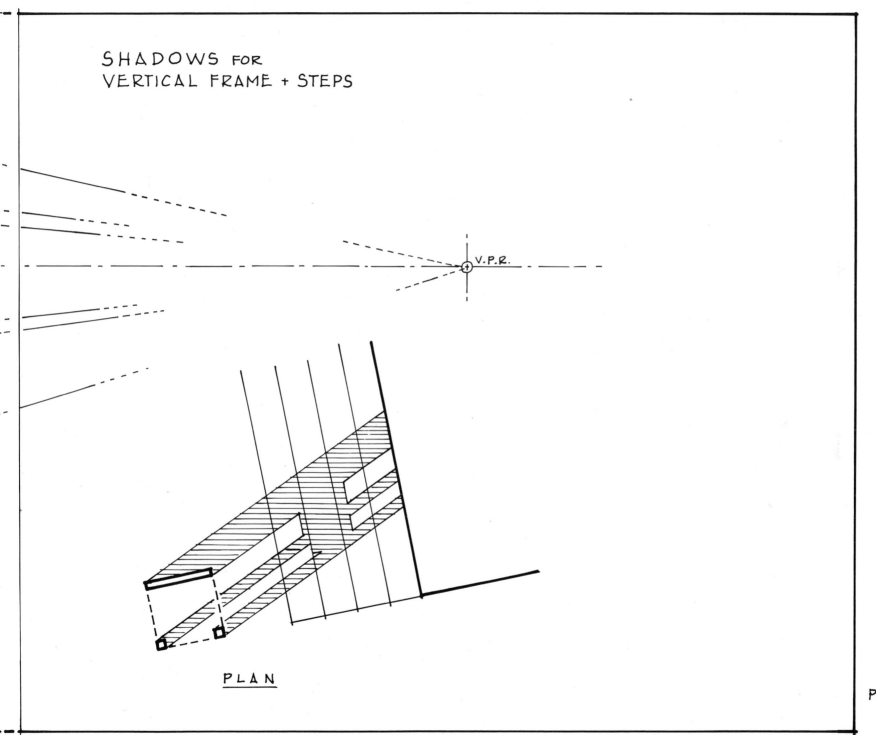

SHADOWS FOR
VERTICAL FRAME + STEPS

V.P.R.

PLAN

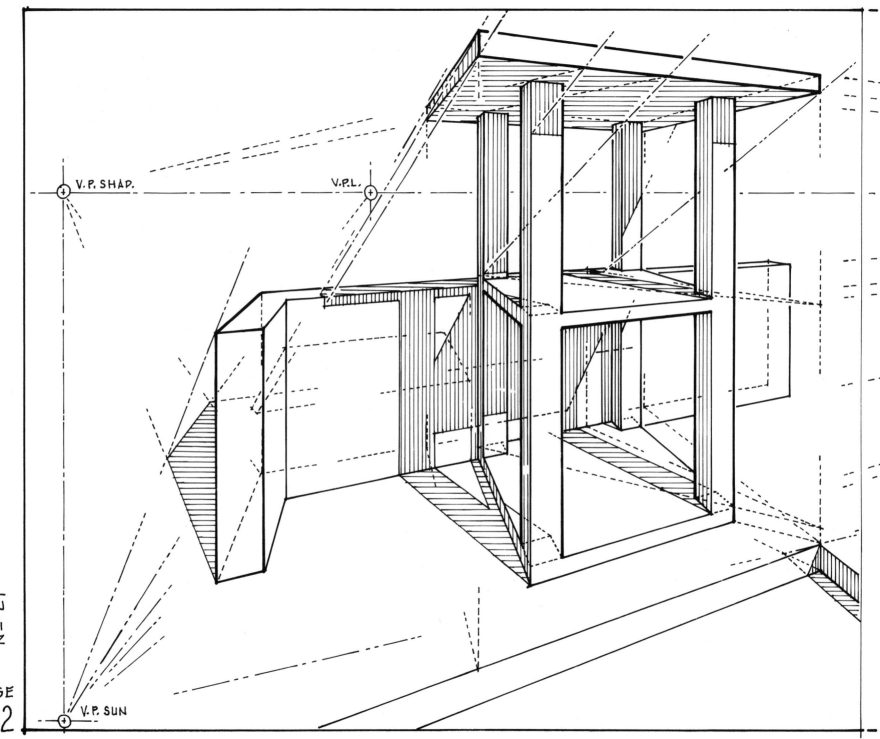

V. P. SHAD.

V.P.L.

STUDY
Nº 29

PAGE
62

V. P. SUN

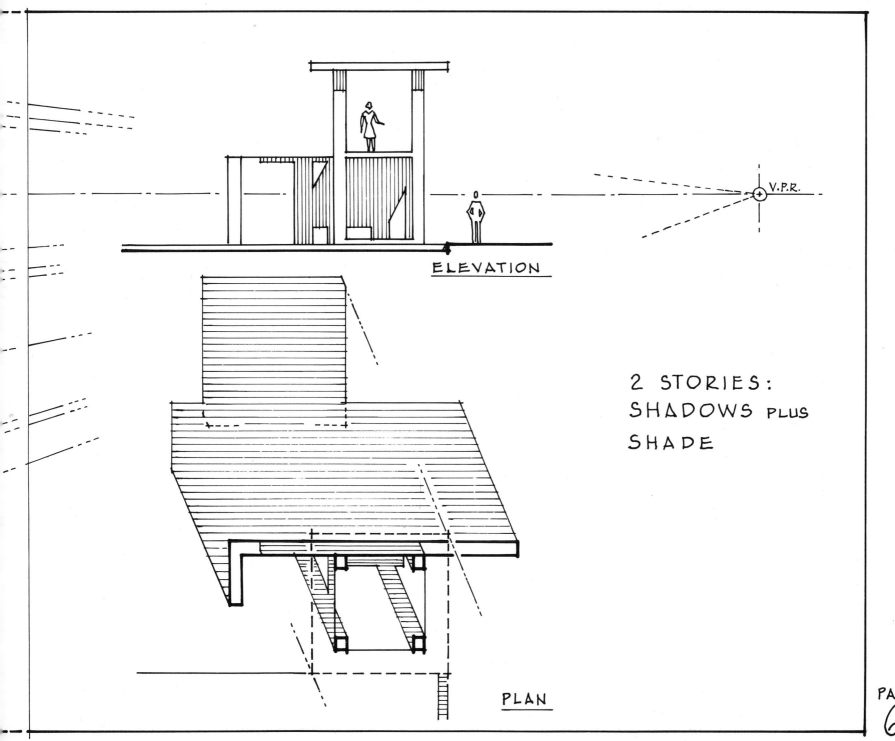

ELEVATION

V.P.R.

2 STORIES:
SHADOWS PLUS
SHADE

PLAN

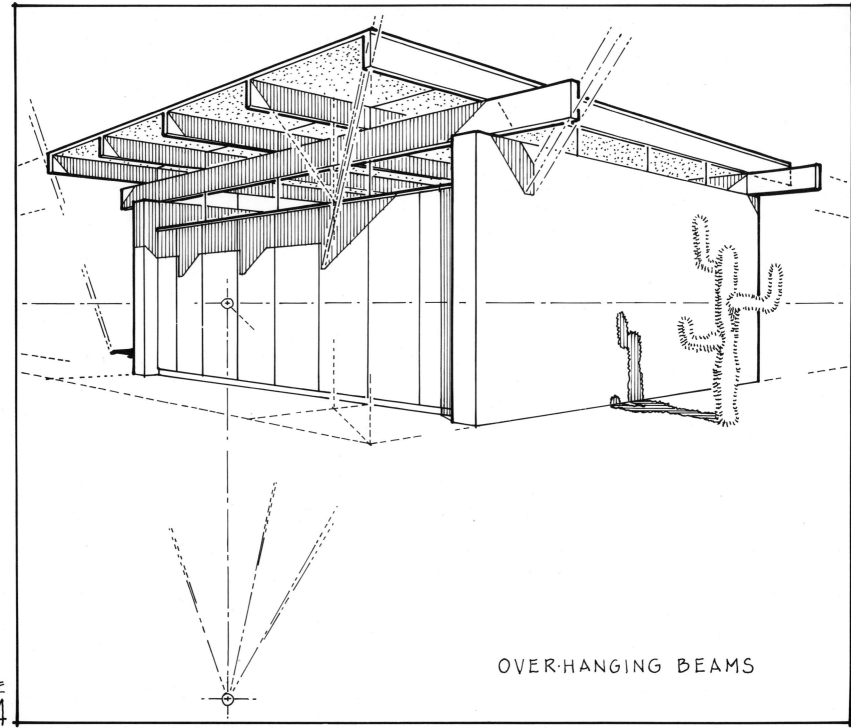

OVER·HANGING BEAMS

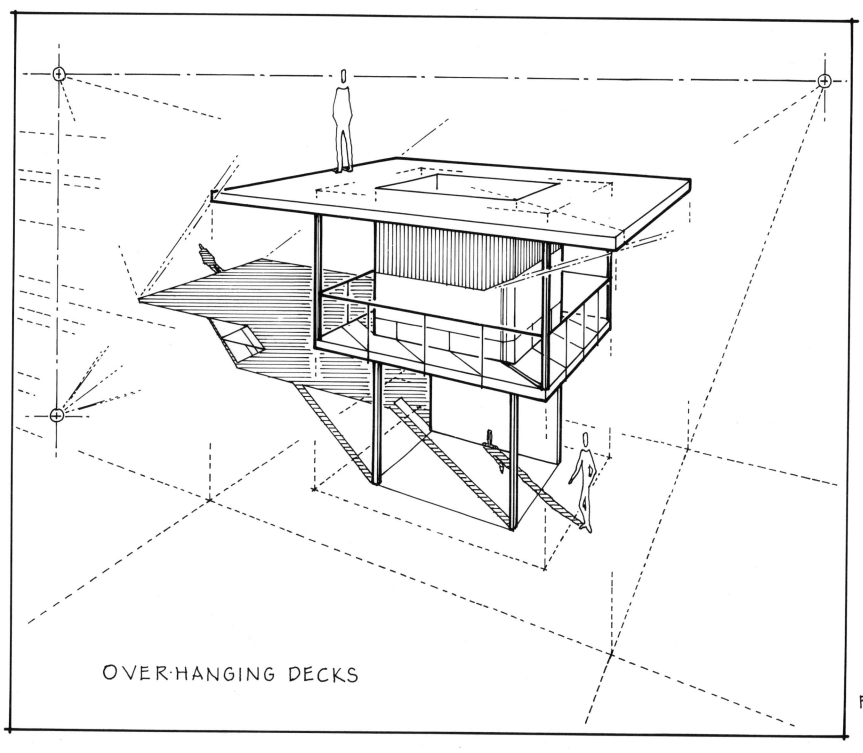

OVER·HANGING DECKS

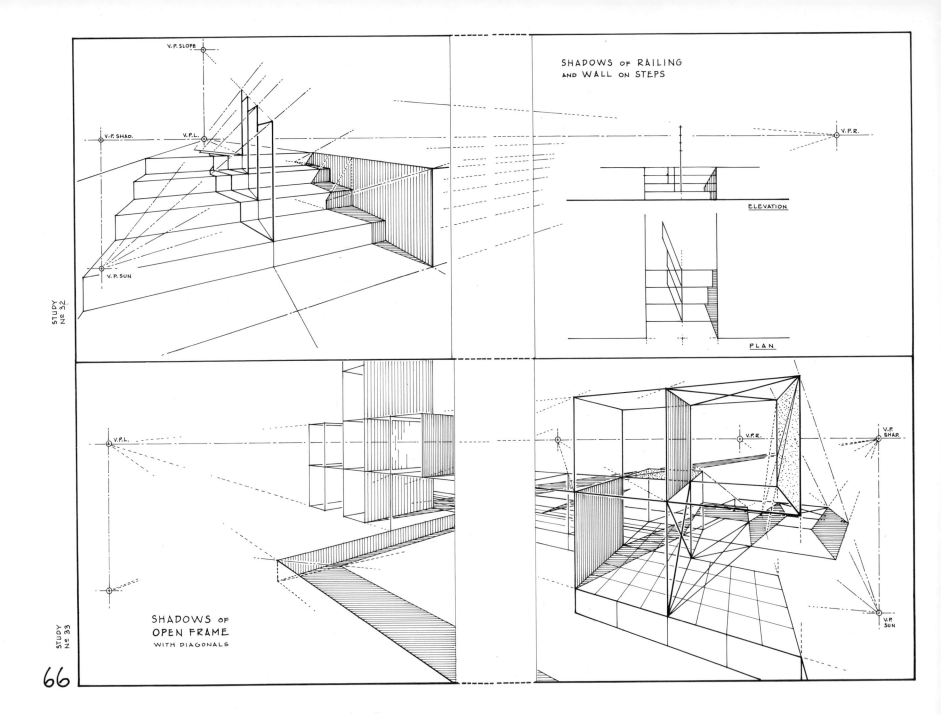

SHADOWS of RAILING
and WALL on STEPS

ELEVATION

PLAN

V.P. SLOPE

V.P. SHAD.

V.P.L.

V.P. SUN

V.P.R.

STUDY Nº 32

V.P.L.

SHADOWS of
OPEN FRAME
WITH DIAGONALS

V.P.R.

V.P. SHAD.

V.P. SUN

STUDY Nº 33

66

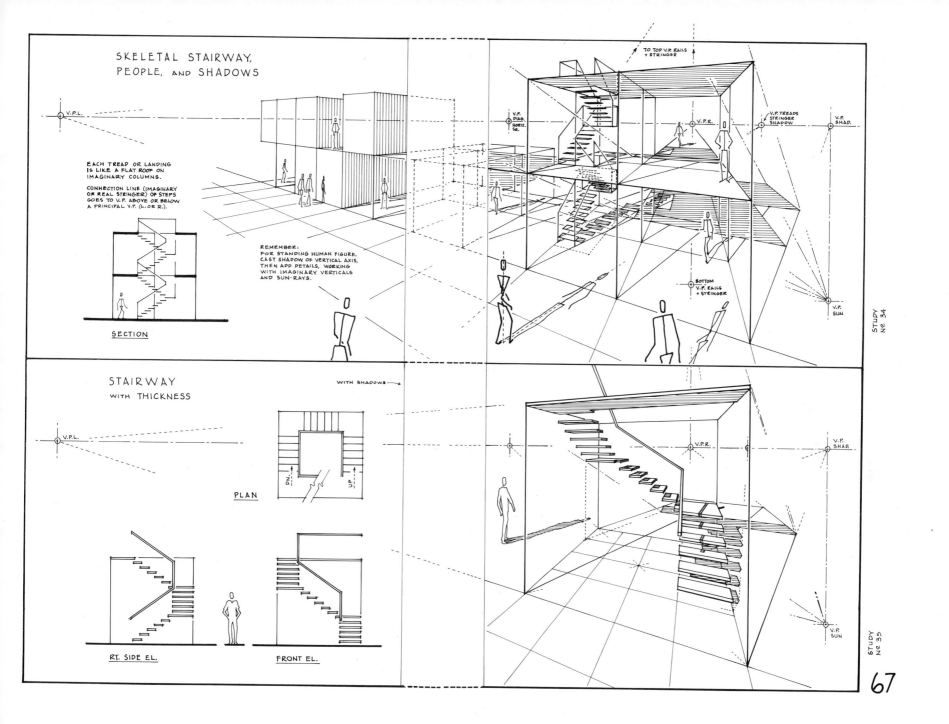

SKELETAL STAIRWAY,
PEOPLE, AND SHADOWS

V.P.L.

EACH TREAD OR LANDING
IS LIKE A FLAT ROOF ON
IMAGINARY COLUMNS.

CONNECTION LINE (IMAGINARY
OR REAL STRINGER) OF STEPS
GOES TO V.P. ABOVE OR BELOW
A PRINCIPAL V.P. (L. OR R.).

REMEMBER:
FOR STANDING HUMAN FIGURE,
CAST SHADOW OF VERTICAL AXIS,
THEN ADD DETAILS, WORKING
WITH IMAGINARY VERTICALS
AND SUN-RAYS.

SECTION

V.P. DIAG.
HORIZ. SR.

TO TOP V.P. RAILS
+ STRINGER

V.P.R.

V.P. TREADS
STRINGER
SHADOW

V.P.
SHAD.

BOTTOM
V.P. RAILS
+ STRINGER

V.P.
SUN

STAIRWAY
WITH THICKNESS

WITH SHADOWS →

V.P.L.

PLAN

DN.

UP

RT. SIDE EL.

FRONT EL.

V.P.R.

V.P.
SHAD.

V.P.
SUN

EXERCISE #7

SHADOWS FOR 2-POINT PERSPECTIVE OF RECTANGULAR FORM

CUT AWAY THE NEXT SHEET AT DASHED LINE ⟶

TAPE THE SHEET TO YOUR DRAWING BOARD.

COMPLETE THE PERSPECTIVE DRAWING WITH MODIFICATIONS INDICATED IN ONE OF THESE VARIATIONS (A,B,C,D) AS ASSIGNED BY YOUR INSTRUCTOR.

THEN, WITH SHADOW OF ROOF CORNER PLACED ON WALL AS SHOWN, FIND FIRST THE VANISHING POINT FOR SHADOWS, NEXT THE VANISHING POINT FOR SUN·RAYS. FINALLY, CONSTRUCT ALL SHADOWS, AND SHOW SHADE AND SHADOW AREAS WITH SPACED·LINE TEXTURES AS USED FOR THE STUDIES.

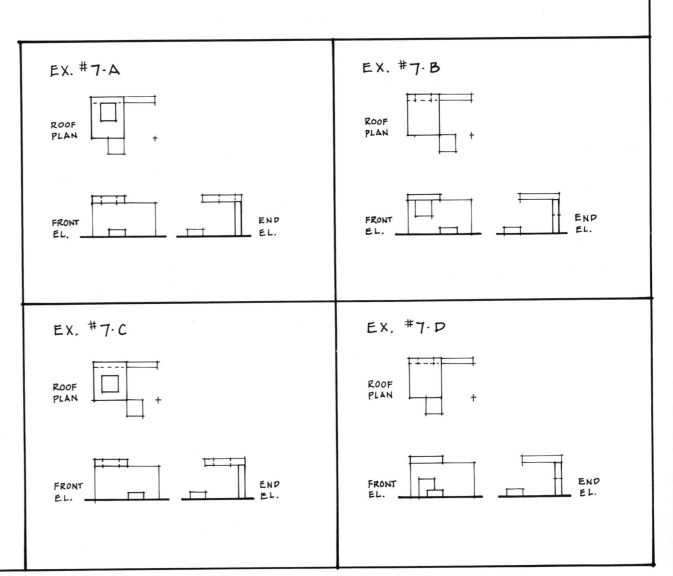

EX. #7·A

ROOF PLAN

FRONT EL.

END EL.

EX. #7·B

ROOF PLAN

FRONT EL.

END EL.

EX. #7·C

ROOF PLAN

FRONT EL.

END EL.

EX. #7·D

ROOF PLAN

FRONT EL.

END EL.

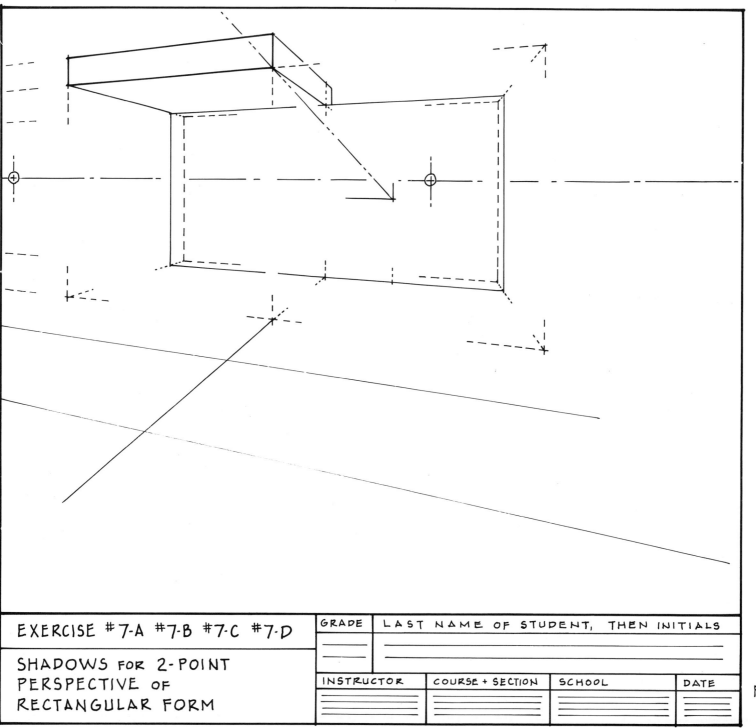

EXERCISE #7-A #7-B #7-C #7-D

SHADOWS FOR 2-POINT
PERSPECTIVE OF
RECTANGULAR FORM

GRADE	LAST NAME OF STUDENT, THEN INITIALS			
INSTRUCTOR	COURSE + SECTION	SCHOOL		DATE

EXERCISE #8

SHADOWS FOR 2-POINT PERSPECTIVE OF RECTANGULAR FORM

TURN OVER YOUR SOLUTION TO EXERCISE #7 AND TRACE LIGHTLY THE BASIC FORM
WITHOUT THE VARIATION THEN ASSIGNED. THE SHADOWS NOW GO BACK LEFT INSTEAD
OF BACK RIGHT. SUBSTITUTE THE NEXT VARIATION IN PERSPECTIVE (A, B, C, OR D)
AND CHANGE THE SHADOWS ACCORDINGLY. EXAMPLE: IF YOU DREW #7-A, NOW
FOR EX. #8, TURN OVER #7 AND MAKE IT #8-B (= #7-B REVERSED).

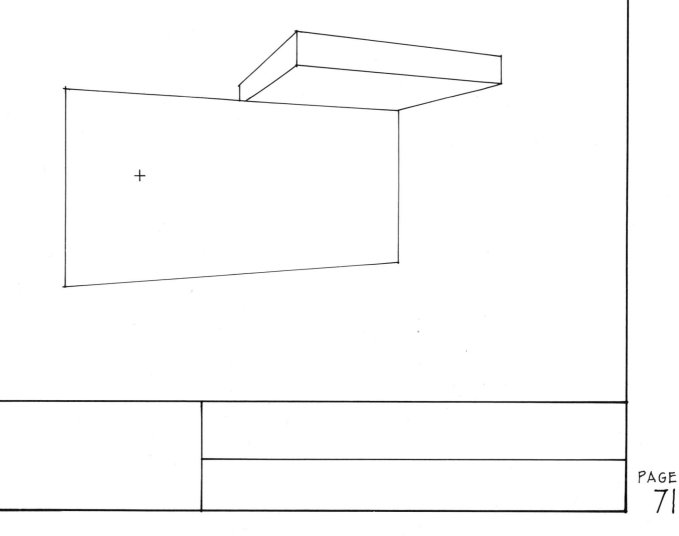

ALSO ON YOUR
TRACING SHEET,
COMPLETE THE
TITLE BOX
WITH ADJUSTED
INFORMATION.

(NOT INTENDED TO
BE CUT AWAY)

SHADOWS FOR
ODD-ANGULAR PLANS
WITH VERTICAL WALLS

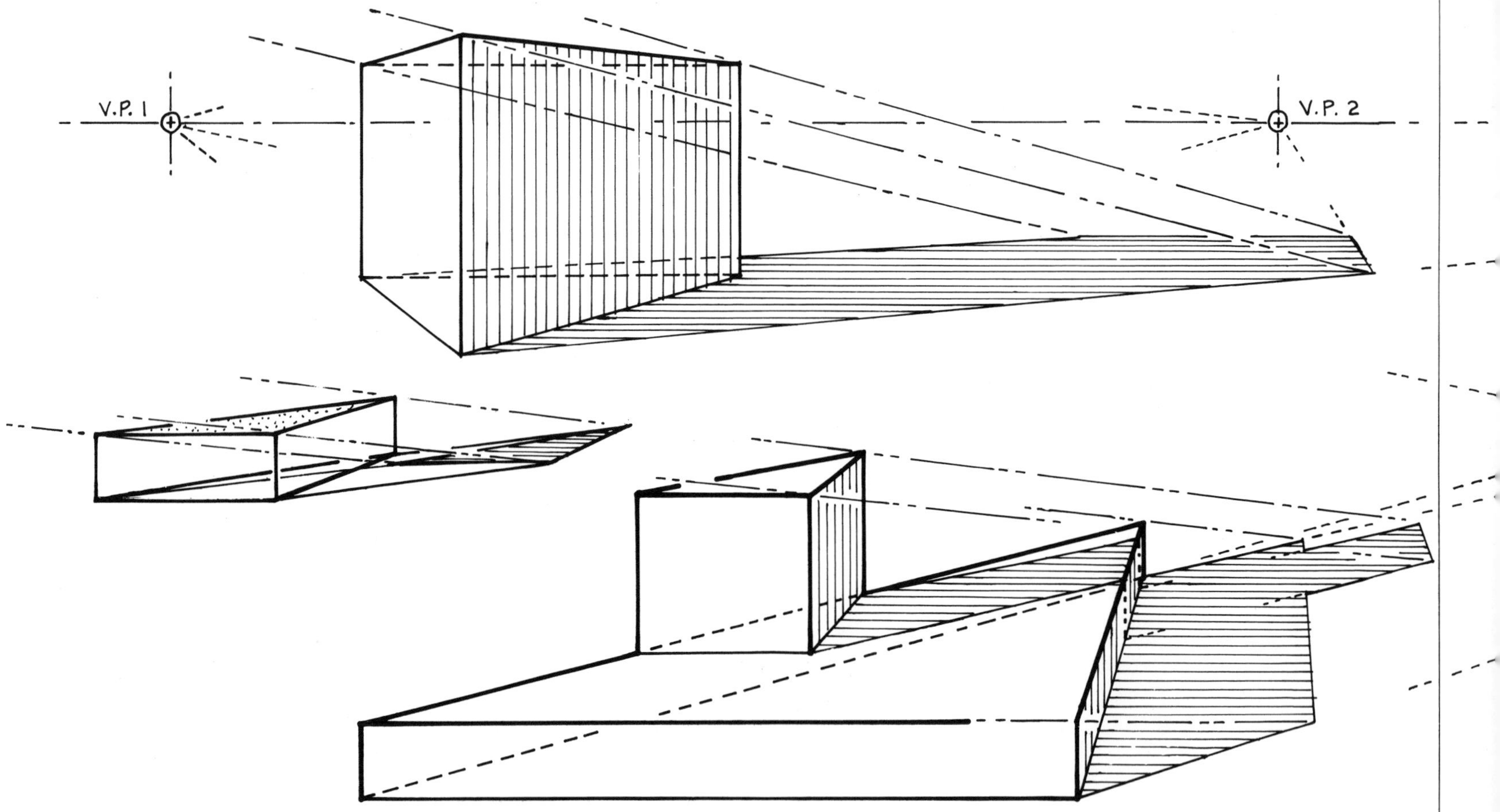

V.P. 1

V.P. 2

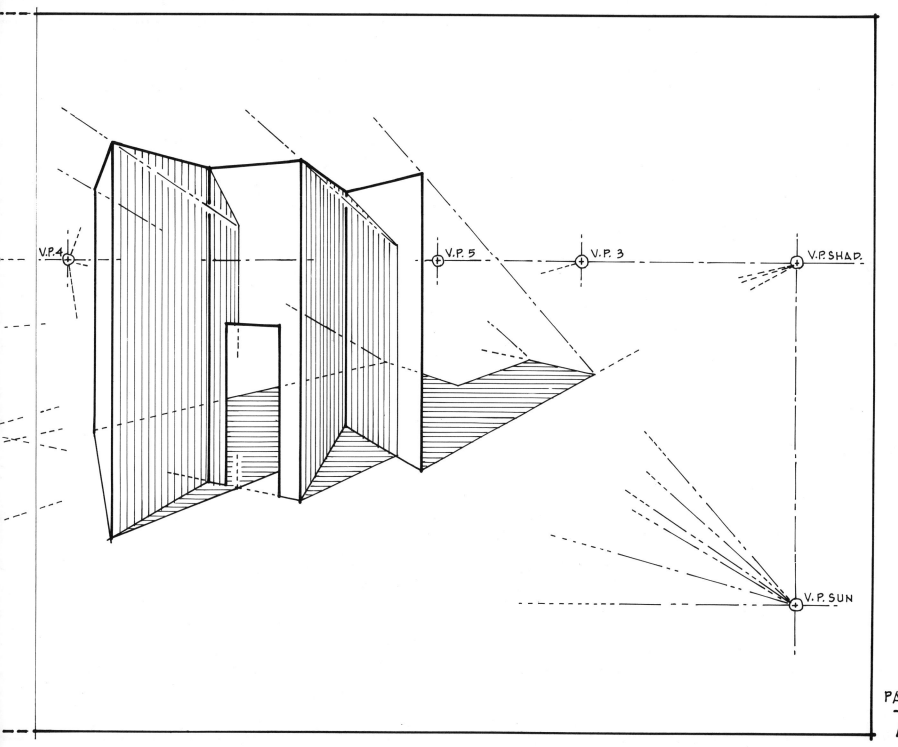

V.P.4

V.P.5

V.P.3

V.P.SHAD.

V.P.SUN

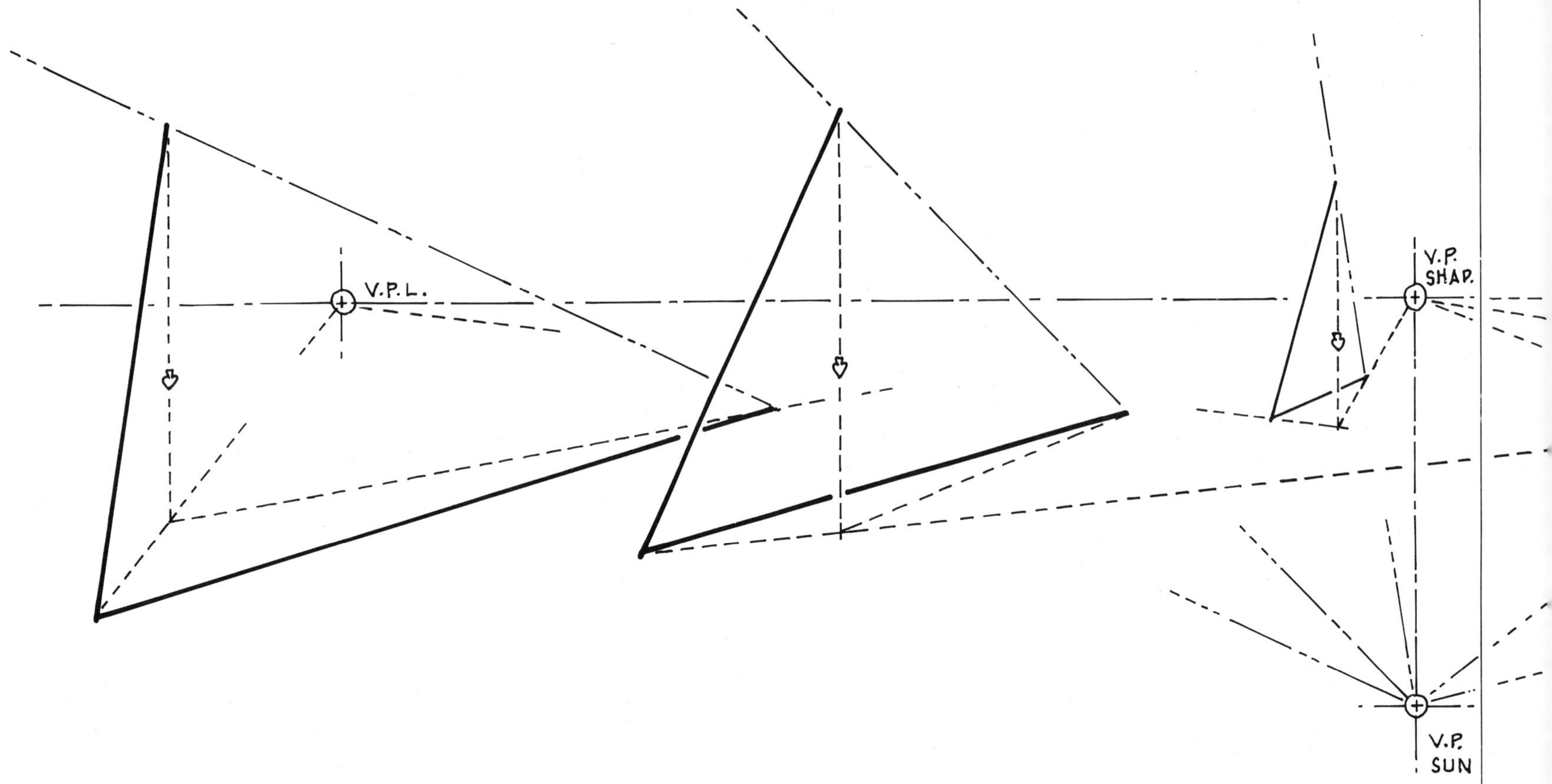

SHADOWS of INCLINED LINES

(SEPARATE, FREE-STANDING)

DROP PLUMB-LINE FROM TOP TO GROUND, THEN
LOCATE ITS IMAGINARY SHADOW, WHOSE TIP
MUST BE JOINED TO BASE OF INCLINED LINE FOR
REAL SHADOW.

(NOTE THAT REAL SHADOW POINTS TO ITS OWN NEW
VAN. PT., USEFUL IF THERE ARE PARALLEL SHADOWS.)

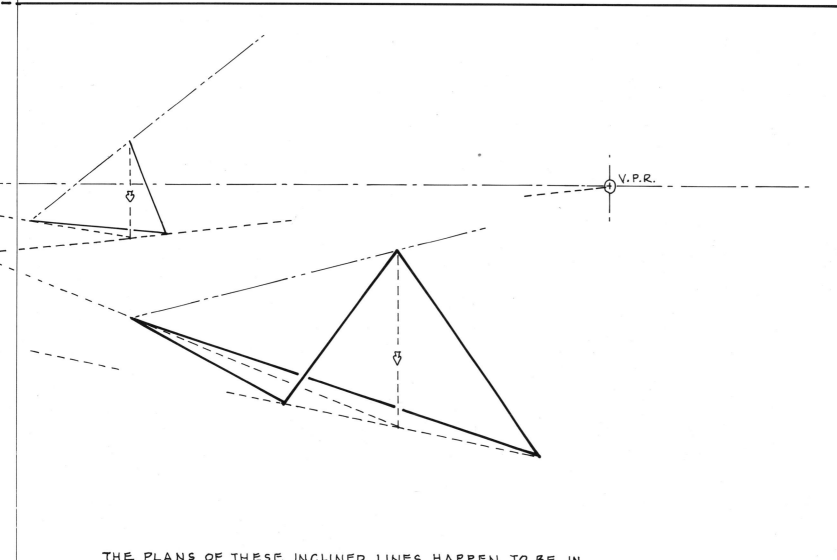

V.P.R.

THE PLANS OF THESE INCLINED LINES HAPPEN TO BE IN
RECTILINEAR RELATION, USING FAMILIAR VANISHING POINTS,
BUT OF COURSE ANY OTHERWISE-DIRECTED INCLINED LINES
WOULD PRODUCE SHADOWS BY LIKE PROCEDURE.

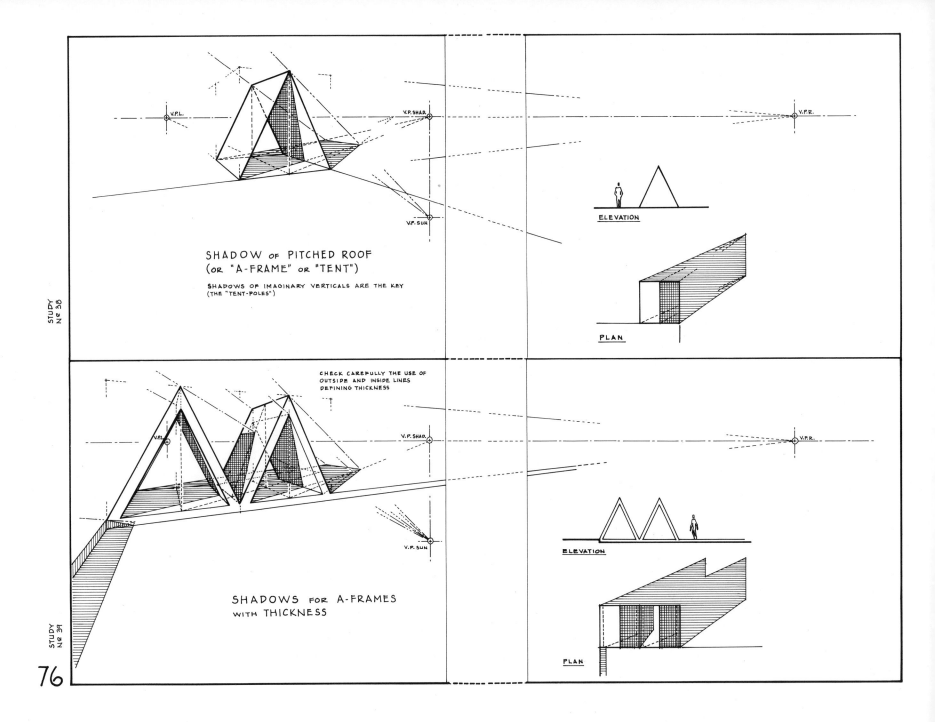

SHADOW of PITCHED ROOF
(or "A-FRAME" or "TENT")

SHADOWS OF IMAGINARY VERTICALS ARE THE KEY
(THE "TENT-POLES")

V.P.L.   V.P. SHAD.   V.P.R.

V.P. SUN

ELEVATION

PLAN

CHECK CAREFULLY THE USE OF
OUTSIDE AND INSIDE LINES
DEFINING THICKNESS

V.P.L.   V.P. SHAD.   V.P.R.

V.P. SUN

SHADOWS FOR A-FRAMES
WITH THICKNESS

ELEVATION

PLAN

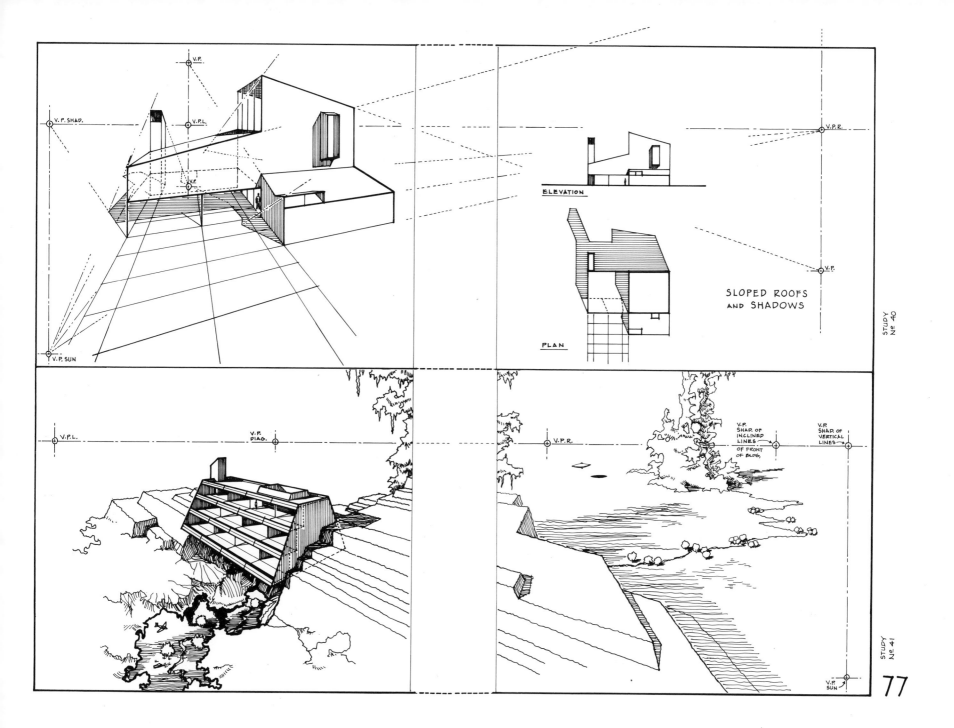

ELEVATION

SLOPED ROOFS
and SHADOWS

PLAN

V.P. SHAD.

V.P.L.

V.P.

V.P. SUN

V.P.

V.P.R.

V.P.

V.P.L.

V.P.
DIAG.

V.P.R.

V.P.
SHAD. OF
INCLINED
LINES
OF FRONT
OF BLDG.

V.P.
SHAD. OF
VERTICAL
LINES

V.P.
SUN

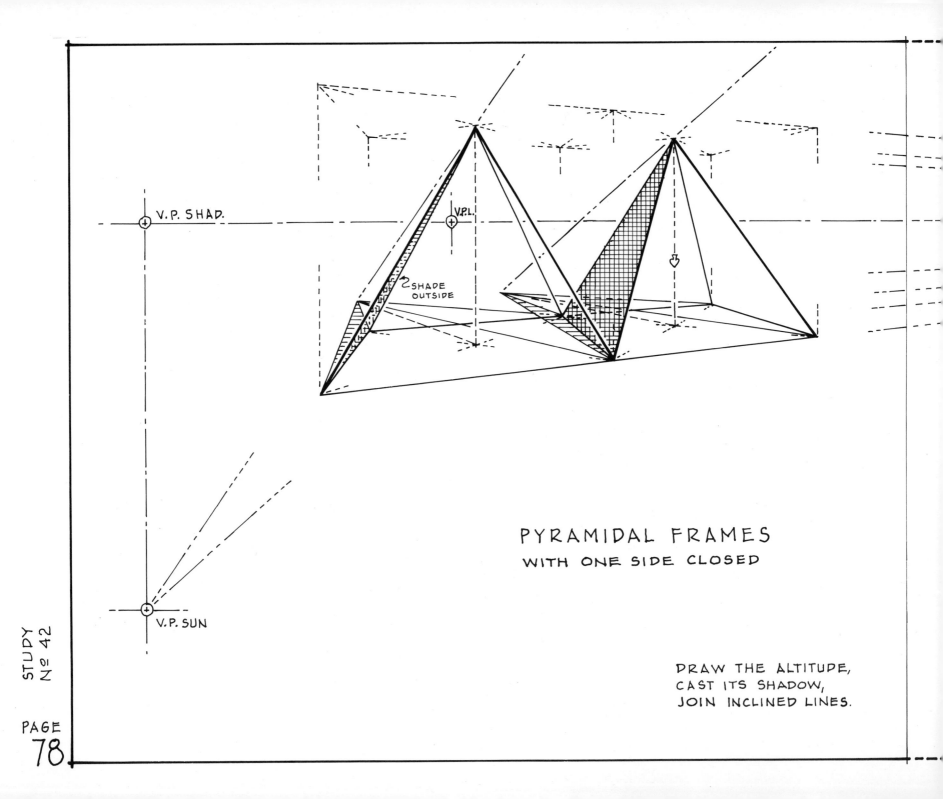

V.P. SHAD.

V.P.L

SHADE OUTSIDE

PYRAMIDAL FRAMES
WITH ONE SIDE CLOSED

DRAW THE ALTITUDE,
CAST ITS SHADOW,
JOIN INCLINED LINES.

V.P. SUN

V.P.R.

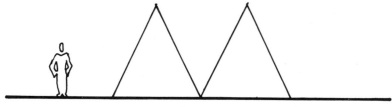

ELEVATION

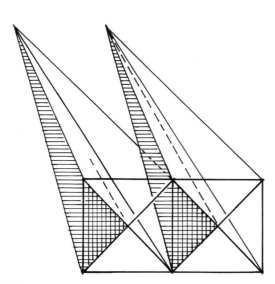

PLAN

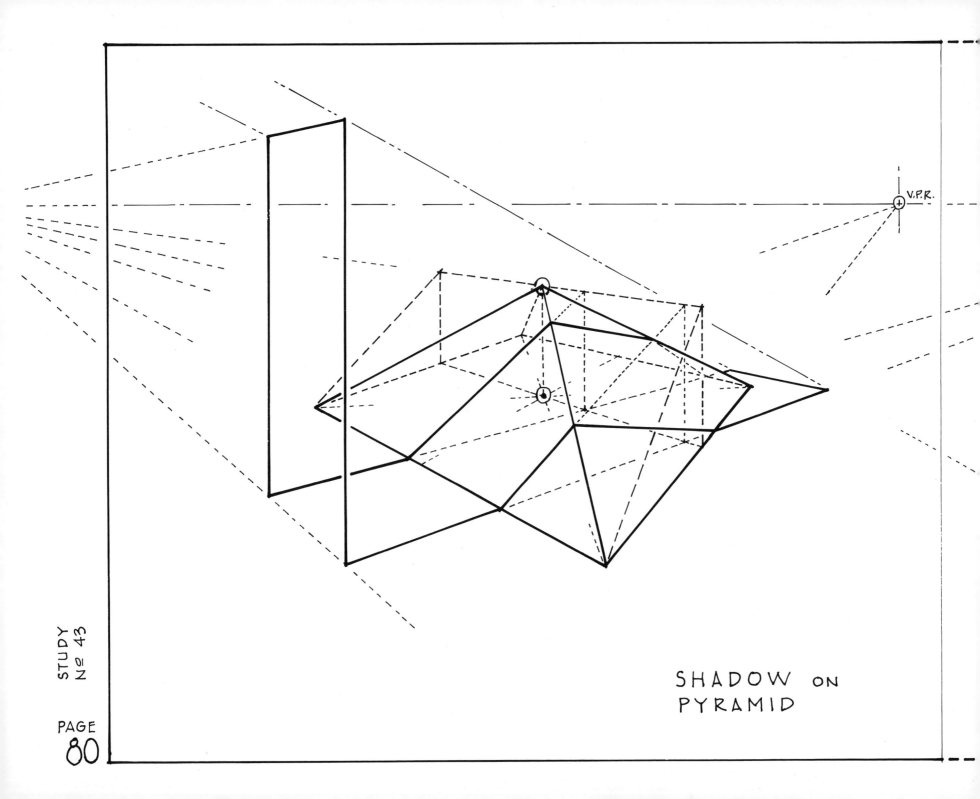

V.P.R.

SHADOW ON
PYRAMID

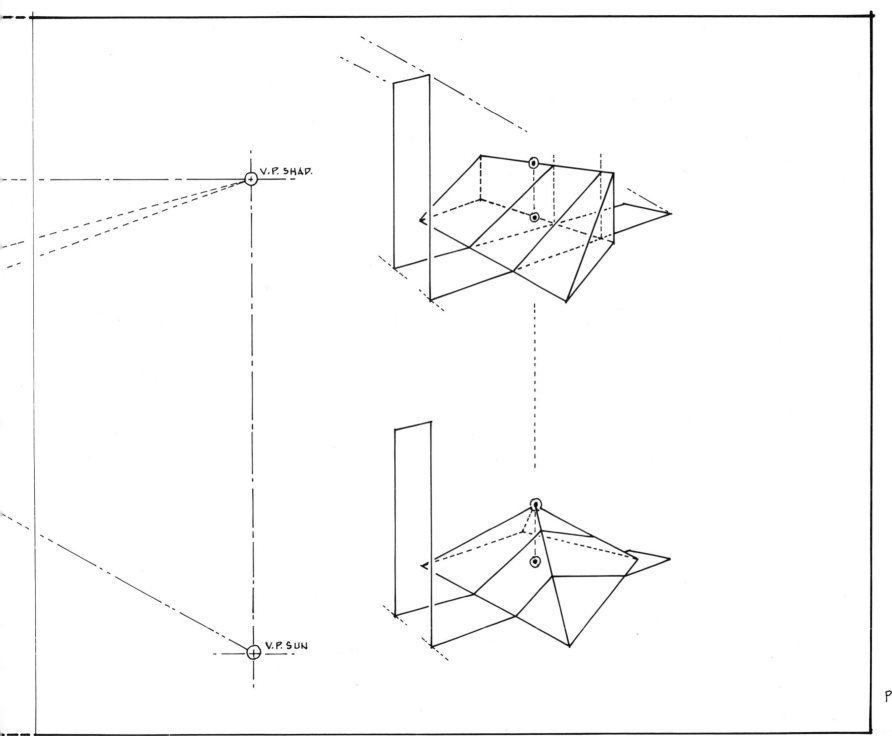

V.P. SHAD.

V.P. SUN

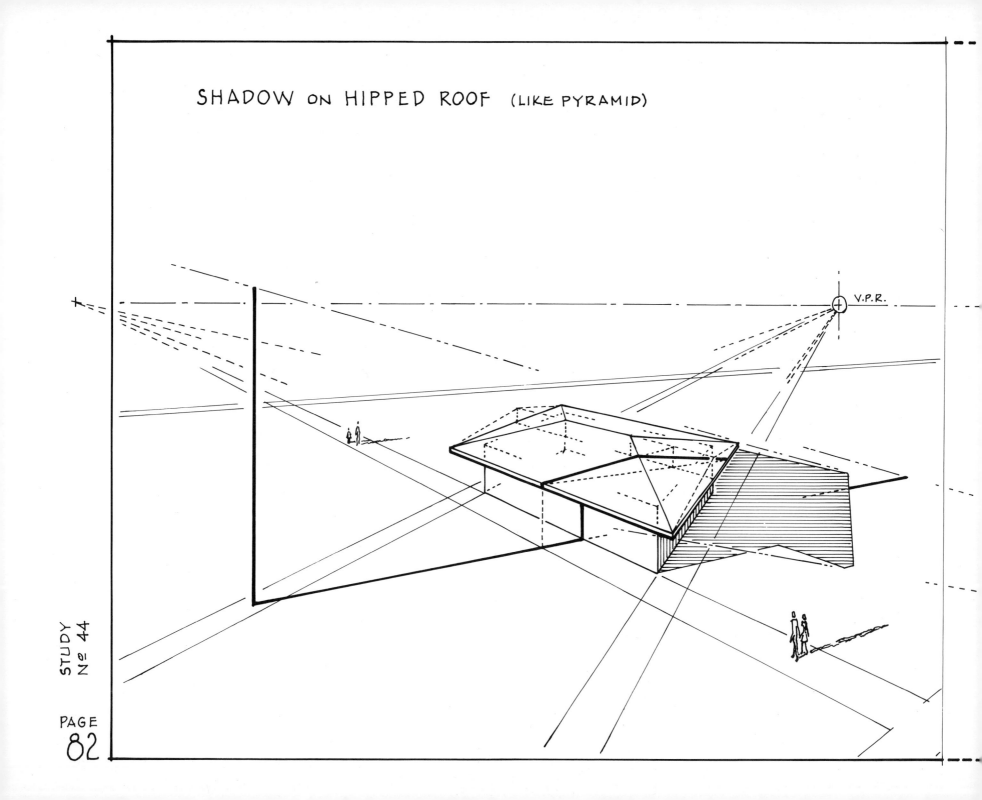

SHADOW ON HIPPED ROOF (LIKE PYRAMID)

V.P.R.

STUDY Nº 44

PAGE 82

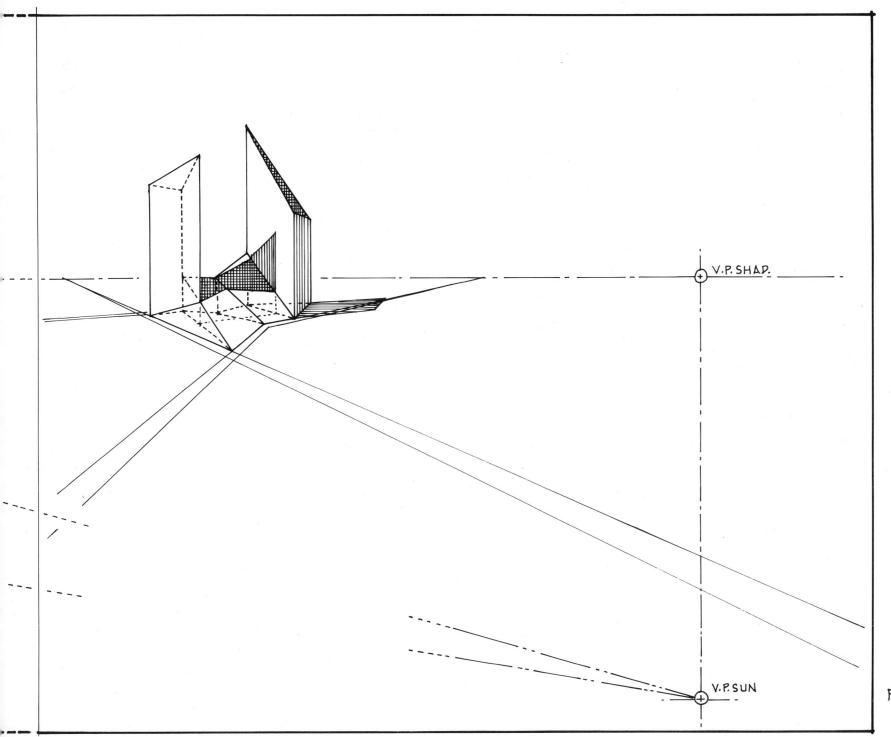

V.P. SHAD.

V.P. SUN

SHADOWS
OF
OCTAGONAL
PLEATED
ROOF

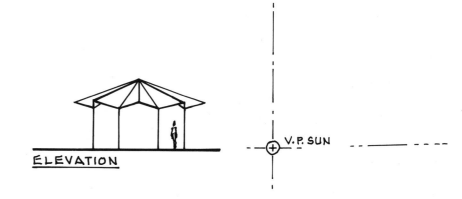

V.P. SHAD.

ELEVATION

V.P. SUN

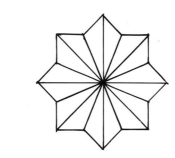

ROOF PLAN

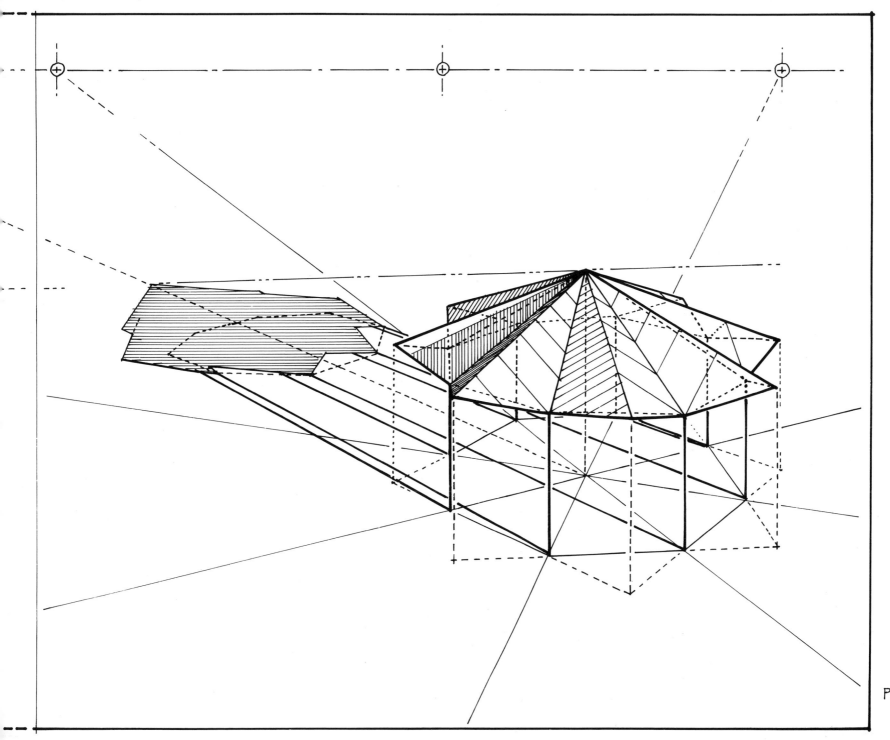

SHADOWS FOR 2-POINT PERSPECTIVE OF ODD-ANGULAR FORM

CUT AWAY THE NEXT SHEET AT DASHED LINE ————————————→
TAPE THE SHEET TO YOUR DRAWING BOARD.

CONSTRUCT ALL
SHADOWS, USING
VANISHING POINT
FOR SHADOWS AS
ALREADY LOCATED.
FOR VANISHING
POINT FOR SUN,
USE ONE OF
THESE LOCATIONS
(A, B, C, OR D)
AS ASSIGNED BY
YOUR INSTRUCTOR.

SHOW SHADE AND
SHADOW WITH
SPACED-LINE
TEXTURE AS
ON STUDIES.

EX. #9-A

LOCATE VANISHING POINT FOR
SUN-RAYS 1½" BELOW
VAN. PT. FOR SHADOWS.

EX. #9-B

LOCATE VANISHING POINT FOR
SUN-RAYS 2½" BELOW
VAN. PT. FOR SHADOWS.

EX. #9-C

LOCATE VANISHING POINT FOR
SUN-RAYS 3" BELOW
VAN. PT. FOR SHADOWS.

EX. #9-D

LOCATE VANISHING POINT FOR
SUN-RAYS 2" BELOW
VAN. PT. FOR SHADOWS.

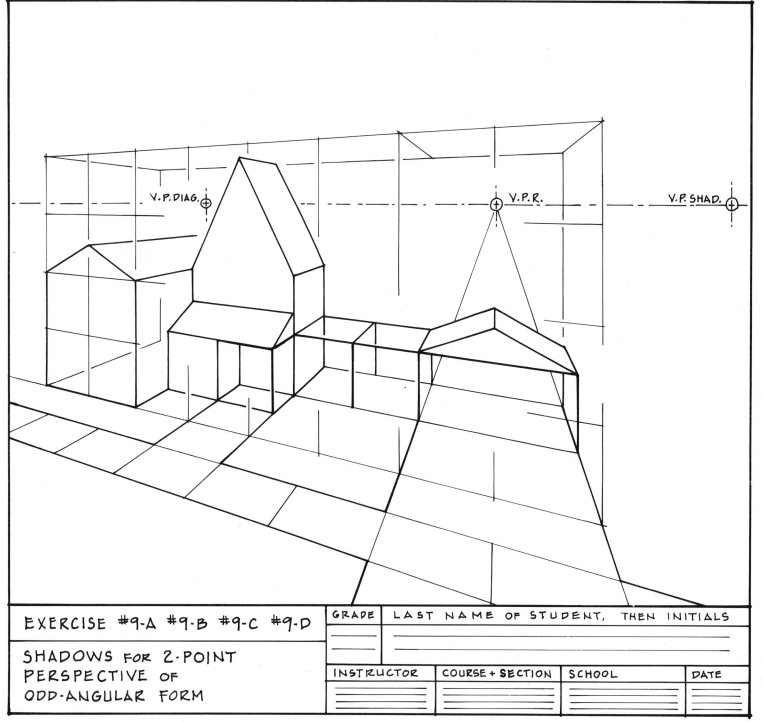

V.P. DIAG.

V.P.R.

V.P. SHAD.

EXERCISE #9-A #9-B #9-C #9-D

SHADOWS FOR 2-POINT
PERSPECTIVE OF
ODD-ANGULAR FORM

GRADE	LAST NAME OF STUDENT, THEN INITIALS

INSTRUCTOR	COURSE + SECTION	SCHOOL	DATE

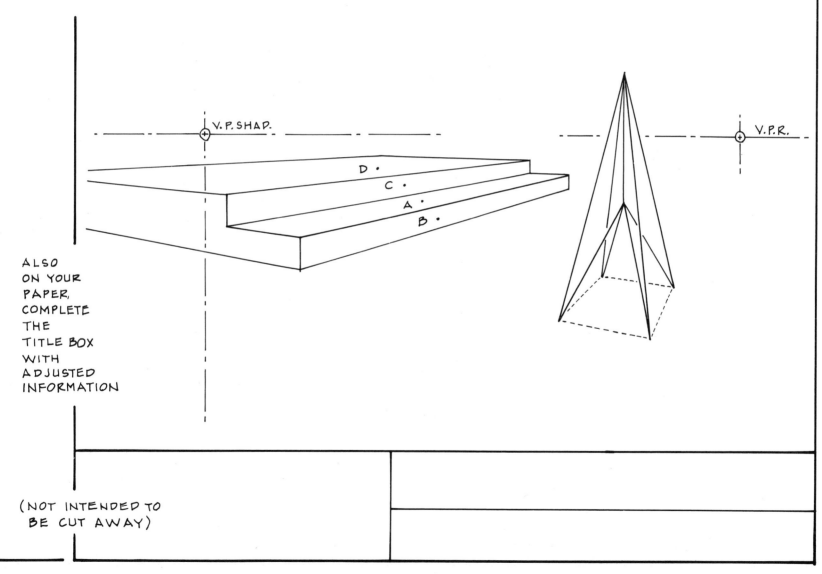

(DO NOT REMOVE THIS SHEET: NEW STUDY ON OTHER SIDE.)

SHADOWS FOR 2-POINT PERSPECTIVE OF ODD-ANGULAR FORM

COPY THIS PERSPECTIVE ON YOUR PAPER. CAST THE SHADOW OF THIS OPEN-FRAME TOWER SO THAT THE APEX FALLS ON POINT A, B, C OR D AS ASSIGNED BY YOUR INSTRUCTOR.

V.P.SHAD.

V.P.R.

D ·
C ·
A ·
B ·

ALSO
ON YOUR
PAPER,
COMPLETE
THE
TITLE BOX
WITH
ADJUSTED
INFORMATION

(NOT INTENDED TO
BE CUT AWAY)

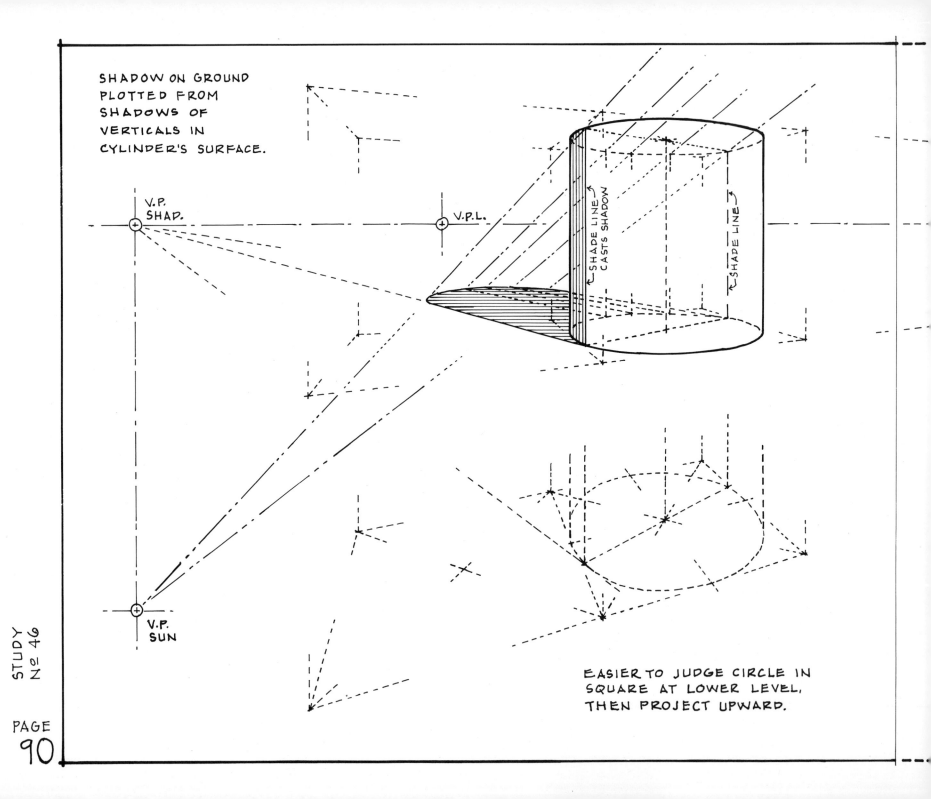

SHADOW ON GROUND
PLOTTED FROM
SHADOWS OF
VERTICALS IN
CYLINDER'S SURFACE.

V.P.
SHAD.

V.P.L.

SHADE LINE
CASTS SHADOW

SHADE LINE

V.P.
SUN

EASIER TO JUDGE CIRCLE IN
SQUARE AT LOWER LEVEL,
THEN PROJECT UPWARD.

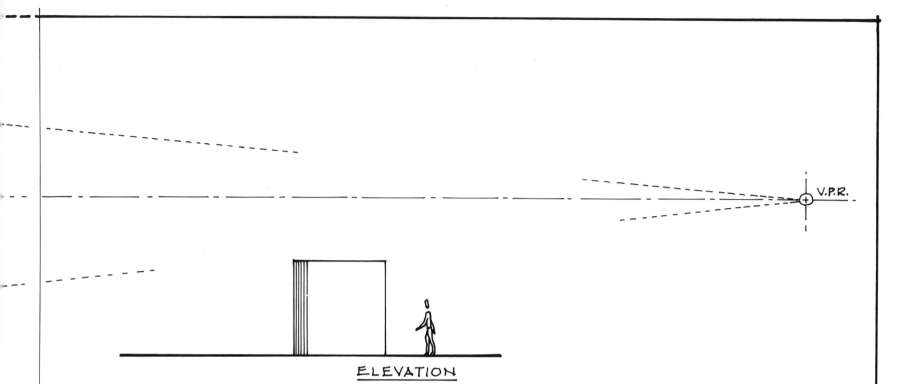

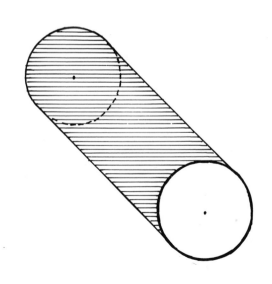

V.P.R.

ELEVATION

PLAN

CURVED FORMS

SHADE AND SHADOW
OF CYLINDER

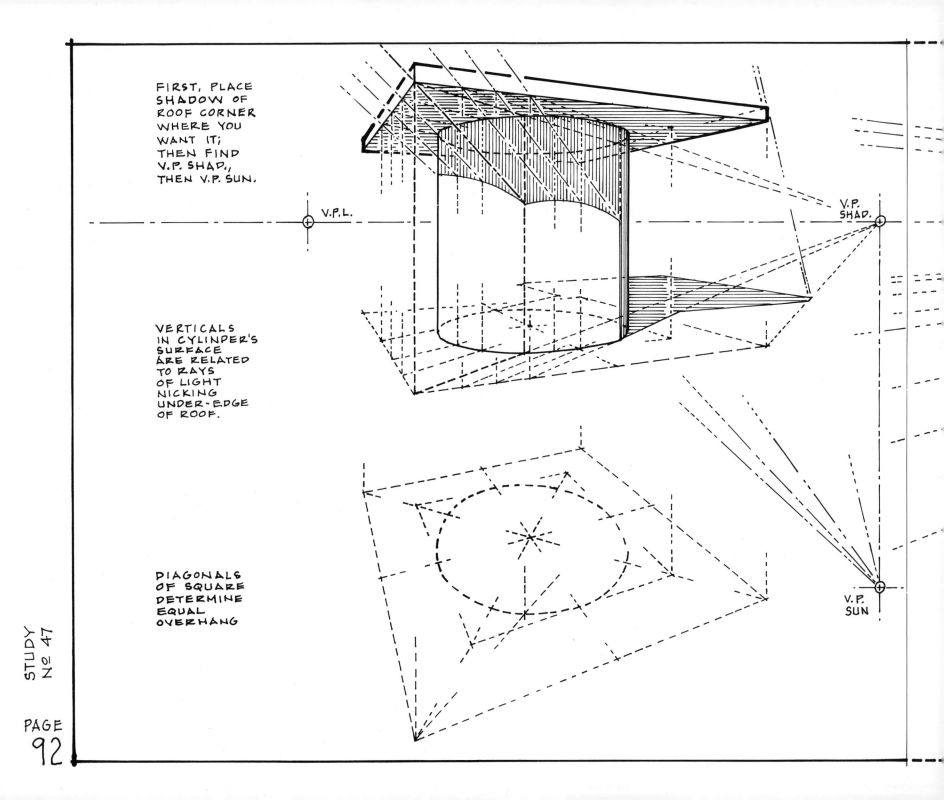

FIRST, PLACE
SHADOW OF
ROOF CORNER
WHERE YOU
WANT IT;
THEN FIND
V.P. SHAD.,
THEN V.P. SUN.

⊕ V.P.L.

V.P.
SHAD. ⊕

VERTICALS
IN CYLINDER'S
SURFACE
ARE RELATED
TO RAYS
OF LIGHT
NICKING
UNDER-EDGE
OF ROOF.

DIAGONALS
OF SQUARE
DETERMINE
EQUAL
OVERHANG

⊕
V.P.
SUN

CYLINDER PLUS SQUARE ROOF

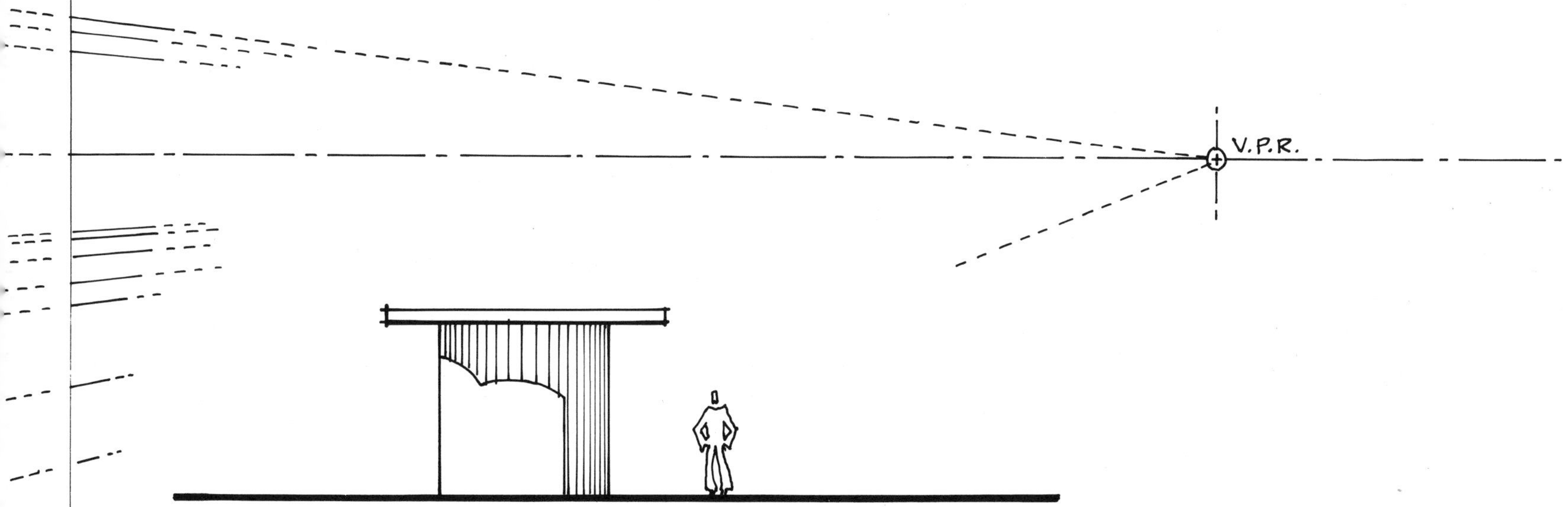

V.P.R.

ELEVATION

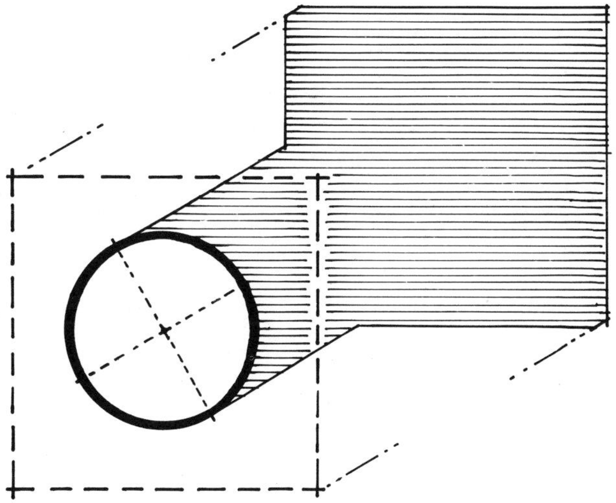

PLAN

CONSTRUCT SHADOW
OF ROOF FIRST,
SHOWING
NOT NECESSARY
TO CAST SHADOW
OF CIRCLE
ATOP CYINDER.

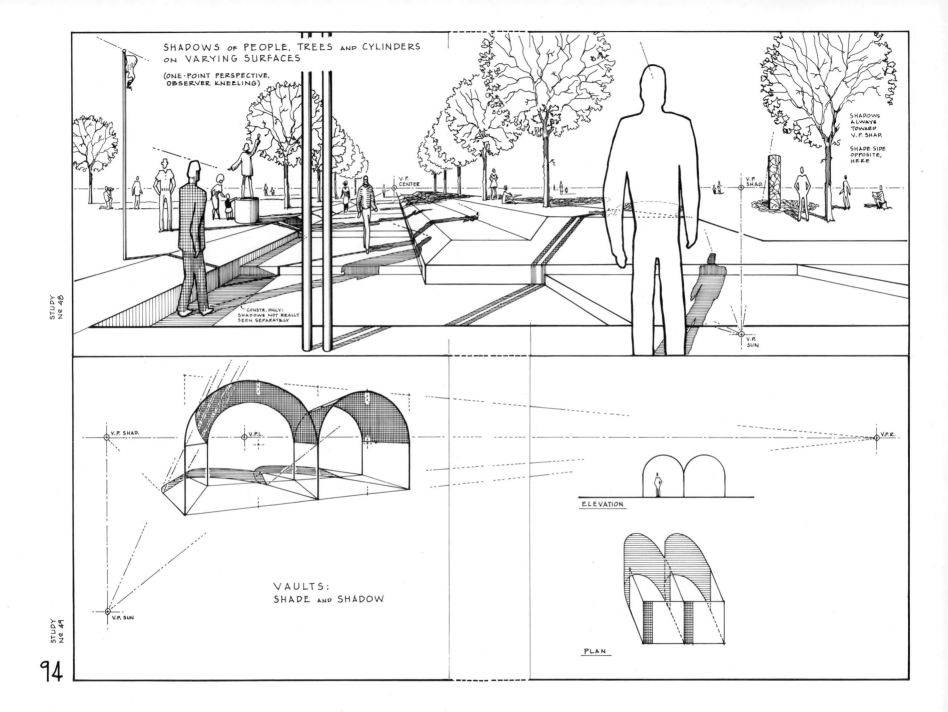

SHADOWS of PEOPLE, TREES and CYLINDERS
on VARYING SURFACES

(ONE-POINT PERSPECTIVE,
OBSERVER KNEELING)

SHADOWS
ALWAYS
TOWARD
V.P. SHAD.

SHADE SIDE
OPPOSITE,
HERE

V.P.
CENTER

V.P.
SHAD.

V.P.
SUN

CONSTR. ONLY:
SHADOWS NOT REALLY
SEEN SEPARATELY

V.P. SHAD.

V.P.L.

V.P.R.

V.P. SUN

VAULTS:
SHADE and SHADOW

ELEVATION

PLAN

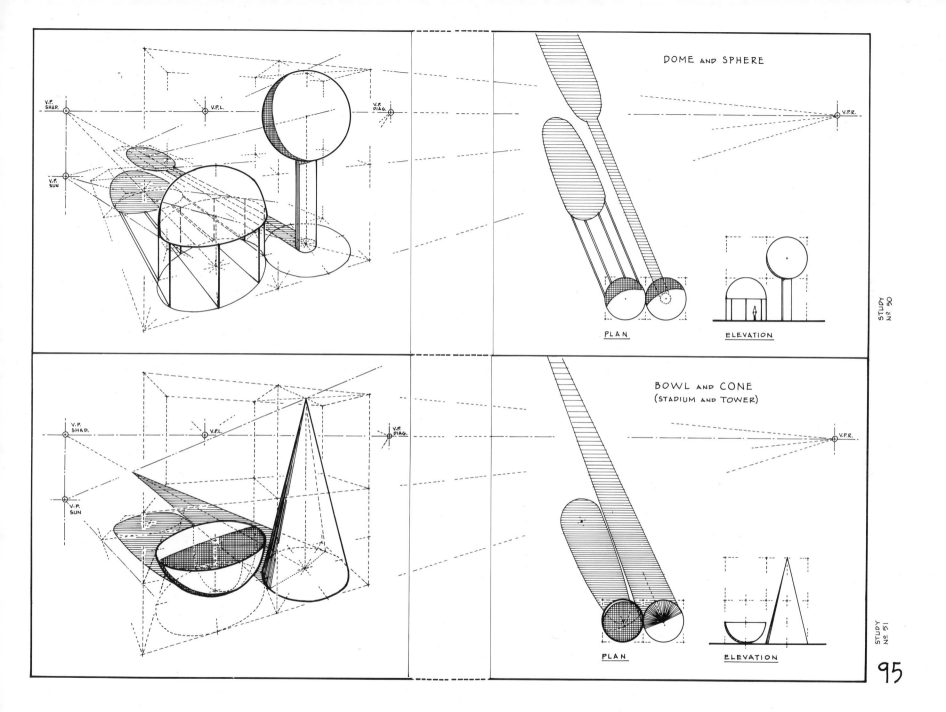

DOME AND SPHERE

PLAN   ELEVATION

BOWL AND CONE
(STADIUM AND TOWER)

PLAN   ELEVATION

V.P. SHAD.   V.P.L.   V.P. DIAG.   V.P.R.

V.P. SUN

95

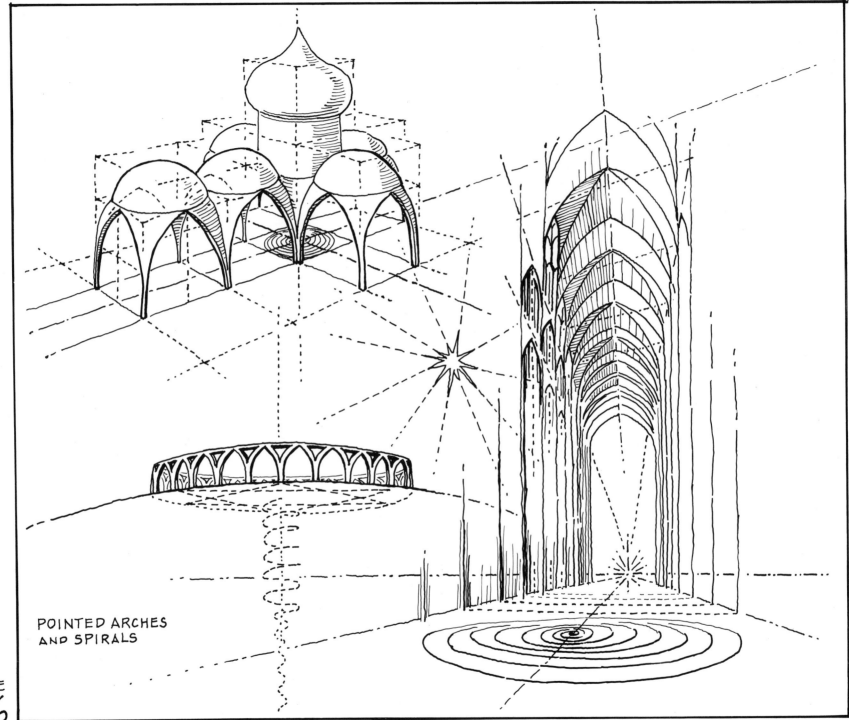

POINTED ARCHES
AND SPIRALS

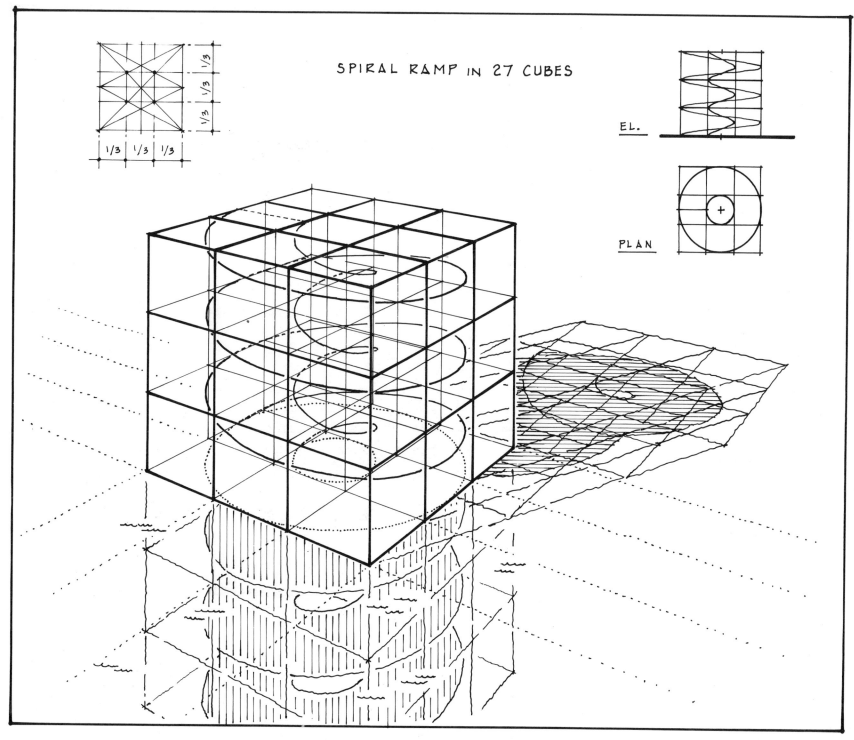

SPIRAL RAMP IN 27 CUBES

EL.

PLAN

1/3 1/3 1/3

1/3
1/3
1/3

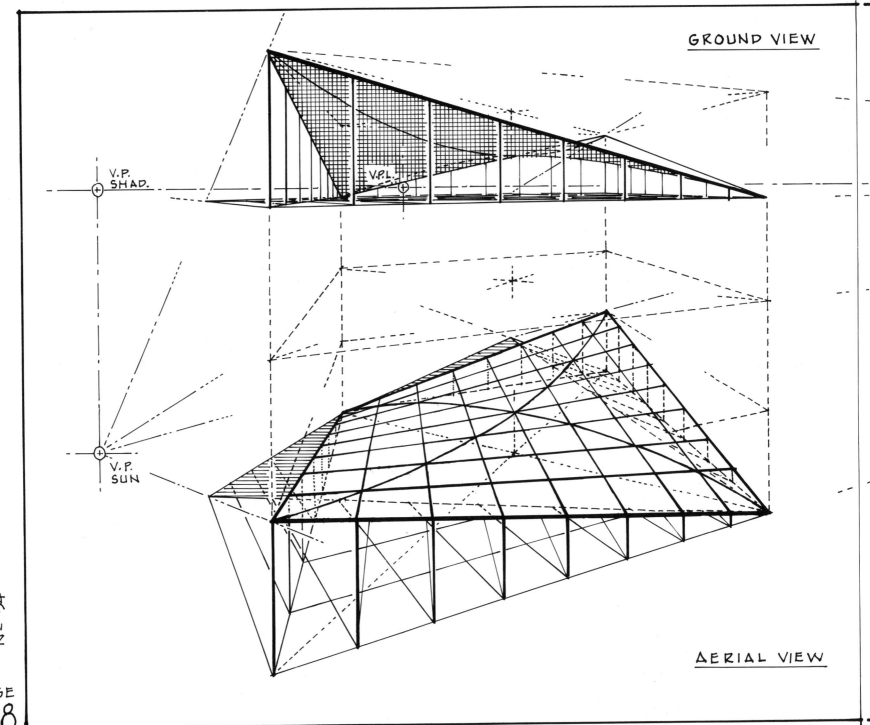

GROUND VIEW

V.P.
SHAD.

V.P.L.

V.P.
SUN

AERIAL VIEW

HYPERBOLIC PARABOLOID

V.P.R.

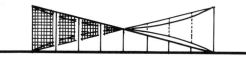

ELEVATION

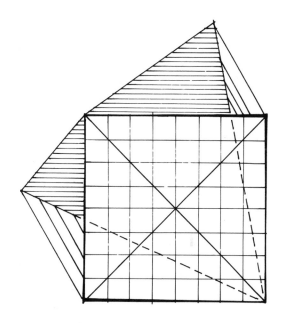

ROOF PLAN + SHADOW

EXERCISE #11

SHADOWS FOR 2-POINT PERSPECTIVE OF CURVILINEAR FORM

CUT AWAY THE NEXT SHEET AT DASHED LINE ————————————→
TAPE THE SHEET TO YOUR DRAWING BOARD.

CONSTRUCT ALL
SHADOWS, USING
VANISHING POINT
FOR SHADOWS AS
ALREADY LOCATED.
FOR VANISHING
POINT FOR SUN,
USE ONE OF
THESE (A,B,C, OR D)
AS ASSIGNED BY
YOUR INSTRUCTOR.

SHOW SHADE AND
SHADOW WITH
SPACED-LINE
TEXTURE, AS
ON STUDIES.

EX. #11-A

LOCATE VANISHING POINT FOR
SUN-RAYS 2" BELOW
VAN. PT. FOR SHADOWS.

EX. #11-B

LOCATE VANISHING POINT FOR
SUN-RAYS 1 1/2" BELOW
VAN. PT. FOR SHADOWS.

EX. #11-C

LOCATE VANISHING POINT FOR
SUN-RAYS 1" BELOW
VAN. PT. FOR SHADOWS.

EX. #11-D

LOCATE VANISHING POINT FOR
SUN-RAYS 2 1/2" BELOW
VAN. PT. FOR SHADOWS.

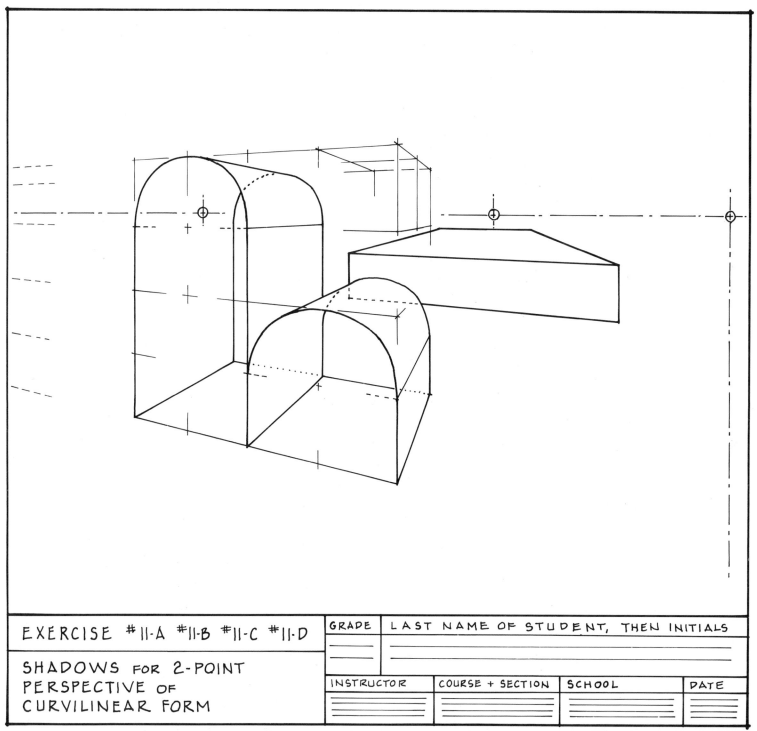

EXERCISE #11-A #11-B #11-C #11-D

SHADOWS FOR 2-POINT
PERSPECTIVE OF
CURVILINEAR FORM

GRADE	LAST NAME OF STUDENT, THEN INITIALS			

INSTRUCTOR	COURSE + SECTION	SCHOOL	DATE

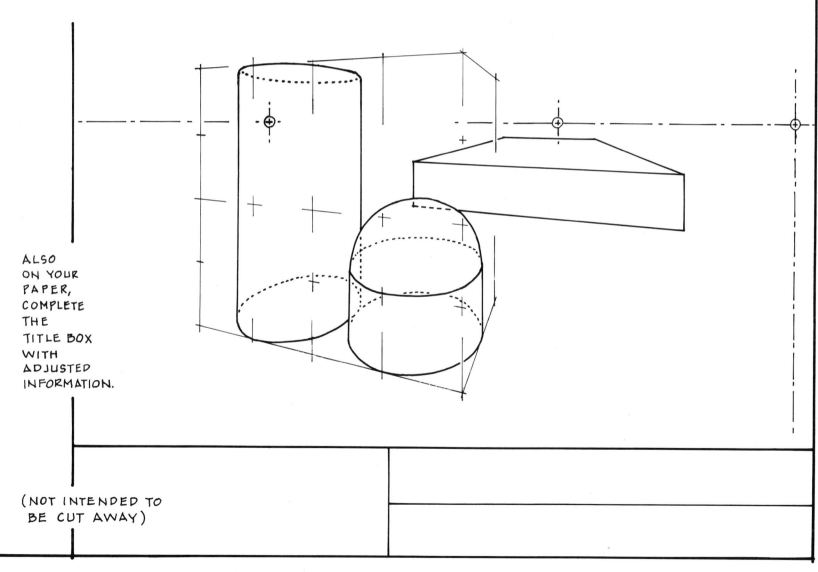

SHADOWS FOR 2-POINT PERSPECTIVE OF CURVILINEAR FORM

USING THE SAME CUBE·MODULE FRAME ON ANOTHER PIECE OF PAPER, CONVERT THE VAULTS OF EX. #11 TO CYLINDER AND DOME. CAST THE SHADOWS TO THE SAME VANISHING POINTS AS IN EX. #11.

ALSO
ON YOUR
PAPER,
COMPLETE
THE
TITLE BOX
WITH
ADJUSTED
INFORMATION.

(NOT INTENDED TO
BE CUT AWAY)

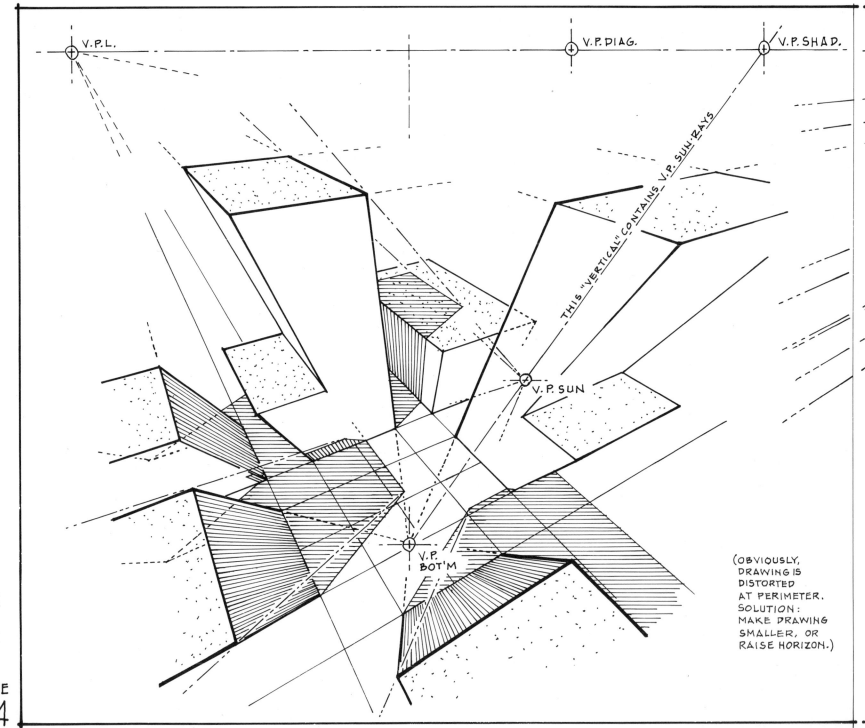

V.P.L.

V.P.DIAG.

V.P.SHAD.

THIS "VERTICAL" CONTAINS V.P. SUN RAYS

V.P. SUN

V.P.
BOT'M

(OBVIOUSLY,
DRAWING IS
DISTORTED
AT PERIMETER.
SOLUTION:
MAKE DRAWING
SMALLER, OR
RAISE HORIZON.)

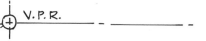

3-POINT PERSPECTIVE
"VAN. PT. BOTTOM" WITHIN PICTURE: AIRPLANE VIEW

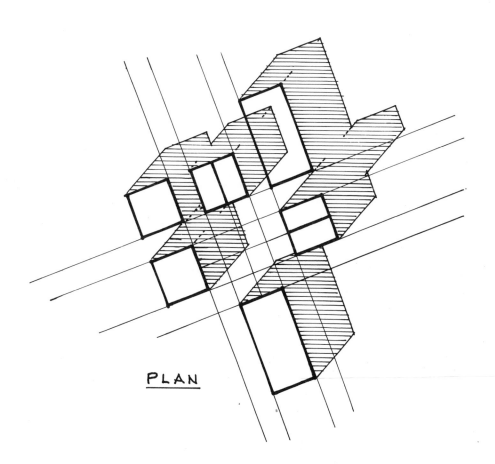

V.P.R.

PLAN

EXERCISE #13

SHADOWS FOR 3-POINT PERSPECTIVE

CUT AWAY THE NEXT SHEET AT DASHED LINE ————————————→
TAPE THE SHEET TO YOUR DRAWING BOARD.

PART OF THE SHADOW HAS BEEN PLACED. FROM THIS, FIND VANISHING POINT FOR SHADOWS AND VANISHING POINT FOR SUN-RAYS. THEN COMPLETE THE SHADOW OF THE VARIATION ASSIGNED BY YOUR INSTRUCTOR: A, B, C, OR D.

ADD TEXTURE (SPACED LINES) FOR SHADOWS.

EX. #13-A

OMIT FROM THE PERSPECTIVE THE CUBE AT LEFT BOTTOM.

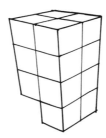

EX. #13-B

OMIT FROM THE PERSPECTIVE THE CUBE AT LEFT, SECOND FROM BOTTOM.

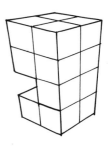

EX. #13-C

OMIT FROM THE PERSPECTIVE THE CUBE AT LEFT, SECOND FROM TOP.

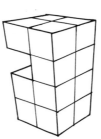

EX. #13-D

OMIT FROM THE PERSPECTIVE THE CUBE AT LEFT TOP.

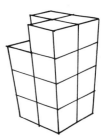

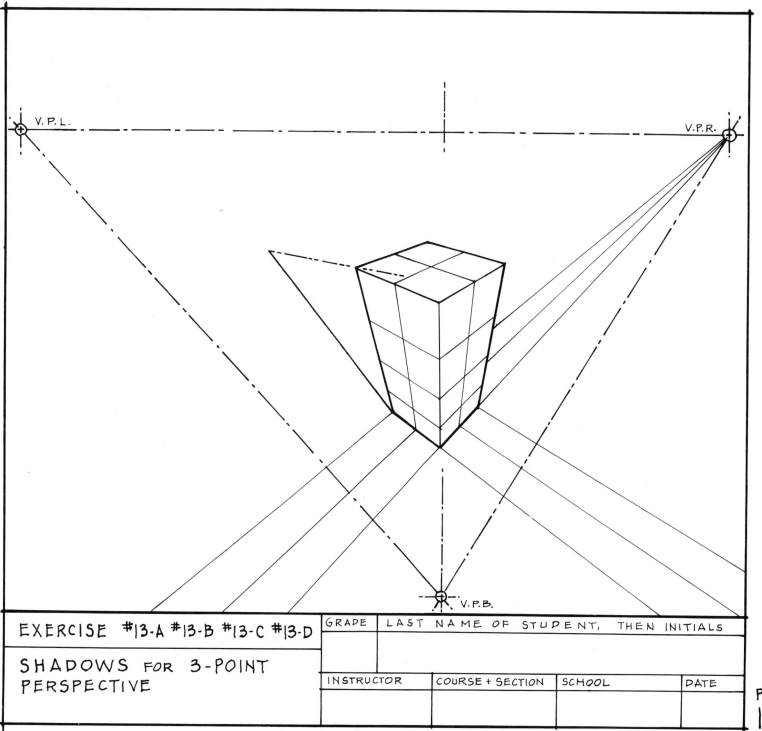

V.P.L.

V.P.R.

V.P.B.

EXERCISE #13-A #13-B #13-C #13-D

SHADOWS FOR 3-POINT PERSPECTIVE

GRADE	LAST NAME OF STUDENT, THEN INITIALS			
INSTRUCTOR	COURSE + SECTION	SCHOOL		DATE

PAGE
107

(DO NOT REMOVE THIS SHEET: NEW STUDY ON OTHER SIDE.)

SHADOWS FOR 3-POINT PERSPECTIVE

TRACE YOUR CUBE-MODULE FRAME OF EXERCISE #13. CHANGE THE FORM
TO THE VARIATION BELOW WHICH HAS THE SAME LETTER: A, B, C, OR D.
CAST THE SHADOWS.

ALSO ON
YOUR PAPER,
COMPLETE THE
TITLE BOX
WITH ADJUSTED
INFORMATION.

EX. #14-A

ALTER AS SHOWN.

EX. #14-B

ALTER AS SHOWN.

EX. #14-C

ALTER AS SHOWN.

EX. #14-D

ALTER AS SHOWN.

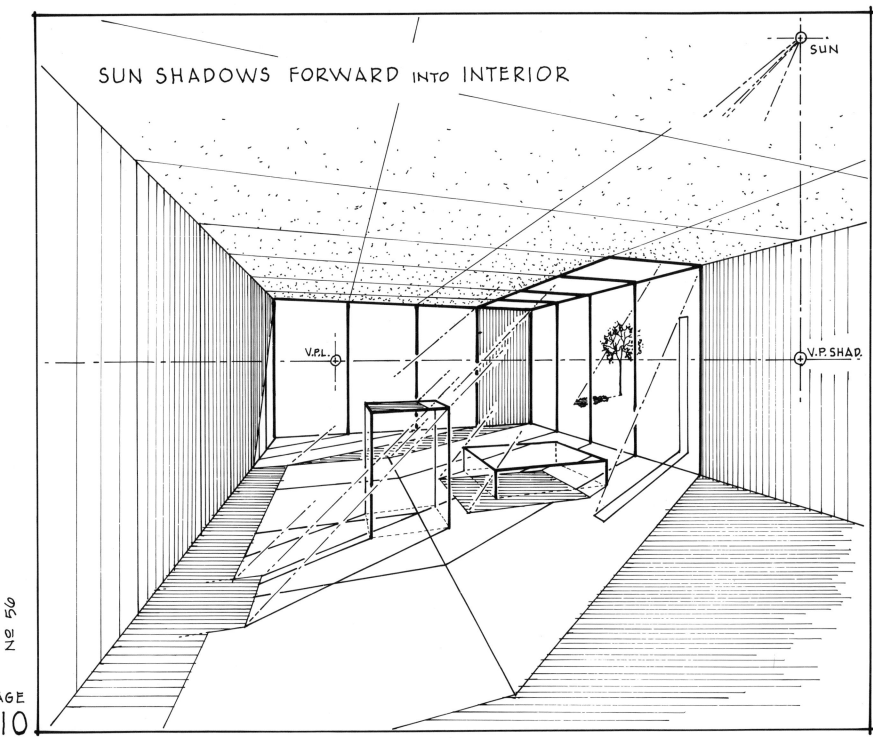

SUN SHADOWS FORWARD INTO INTERIOR

SUN

V.P.L.

V.P. SHAD.

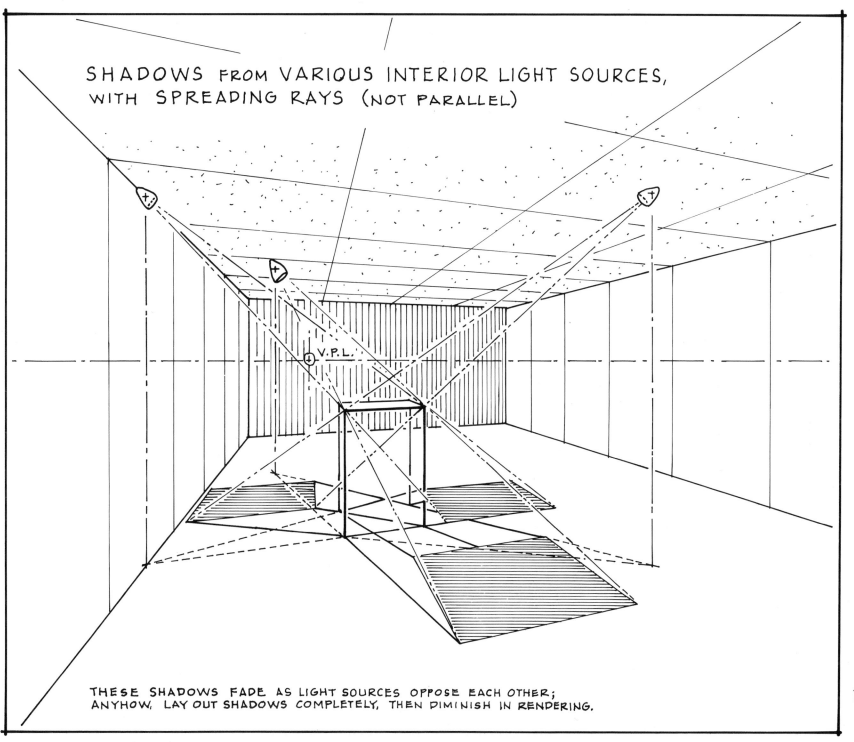

SHADOWS FROM VARIOUS INTERIOR LIGHT SOURCES,
WITH SPREADING RAYS (NOT PARALLEL)

V.P.L.

THESE SHADOWS FADE AS LIGHT SOURCES OPPOSE EACH OTHER;
ANYHOW, LAY OUT SHADOWS COMPLETELY, THEN DIMINISH IN RENDERING.

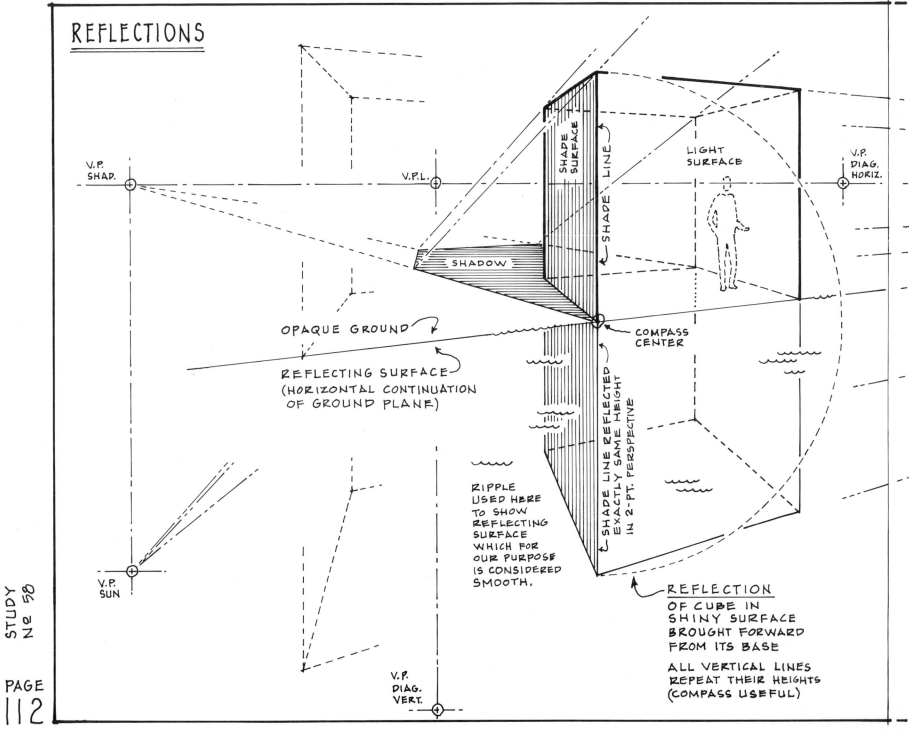

REFLECTIONS

V.P. SHAD.

V.P.L.

LIGHT SURFACE

V.P. DIAG. HORIZ.

SHADE SURFACE

SHADE LINE

SHADOW

COMPASS CENTER

OPAQUE GROUND

REFLECTING SURFACE
(HORIZONTAL CONTINUATION
OF GROUND PLANE)

SHADE LINE REFLECTED EXACTLY SAME HEIGHT IN 2-PT. PERSPECTIVE

RIPPLE
USED HERE
TO SHOW
REFLECTING
SURFACE
WHICH FOR
OUR PURPOSE
IS CONSIDERED
SMOOTH.

V.P. SUN

REFLECTION
OF CUBE IN
SHINY SURFACE
BROUGHT FORWARD
FROM ITS BASE

ALL VERTICAL LINES
REPEAT THEIR HEIGHTS
(COMPASS USEFUL)

V.P. DIAG. VERT.

STUDY No 58

PAGE 112

REFLECTION OF A SOLID CUBE WITH SHADE AND SHADOW

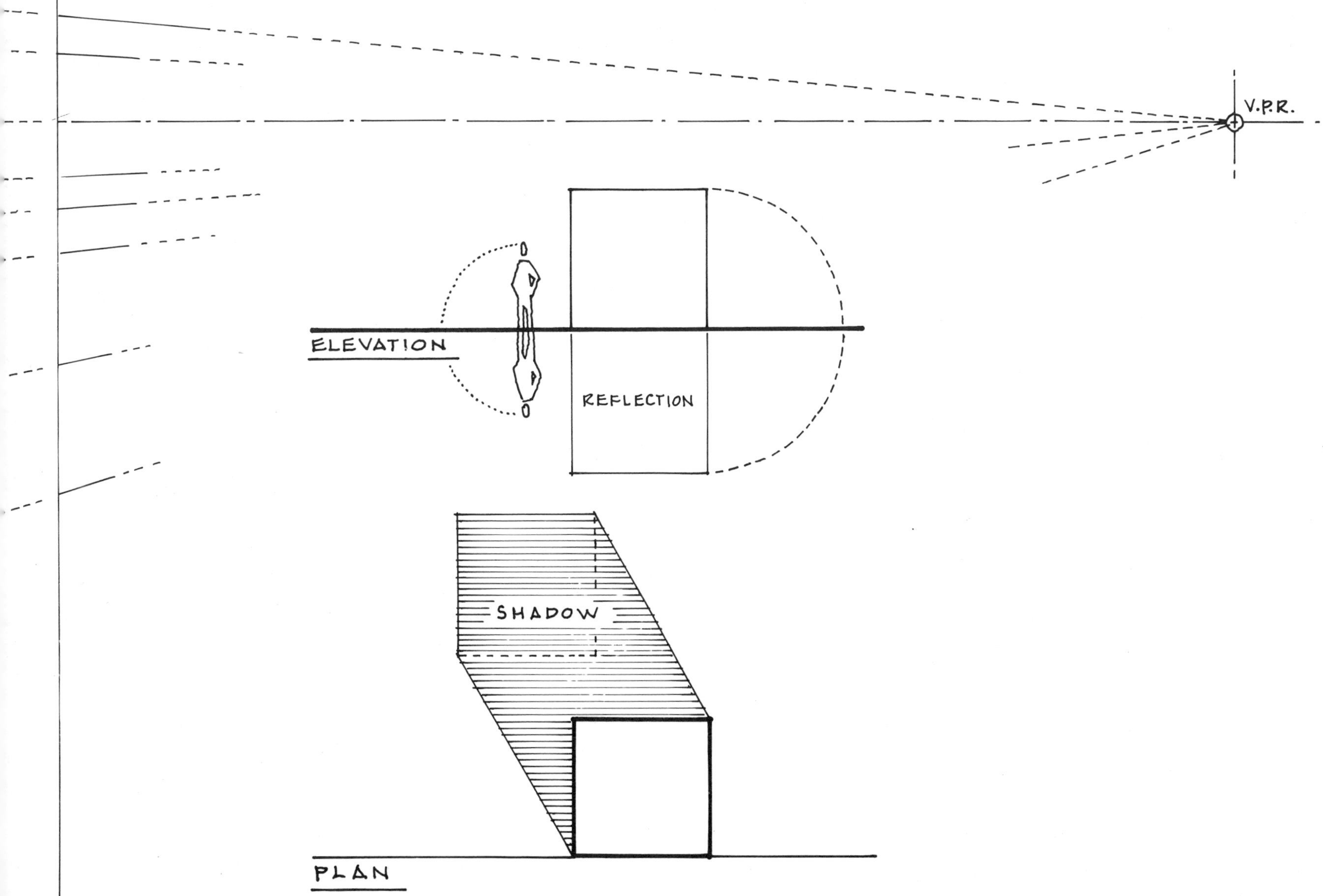

V.P.R.

ELEVATION

REFLECTION

SHADOW

PLAN

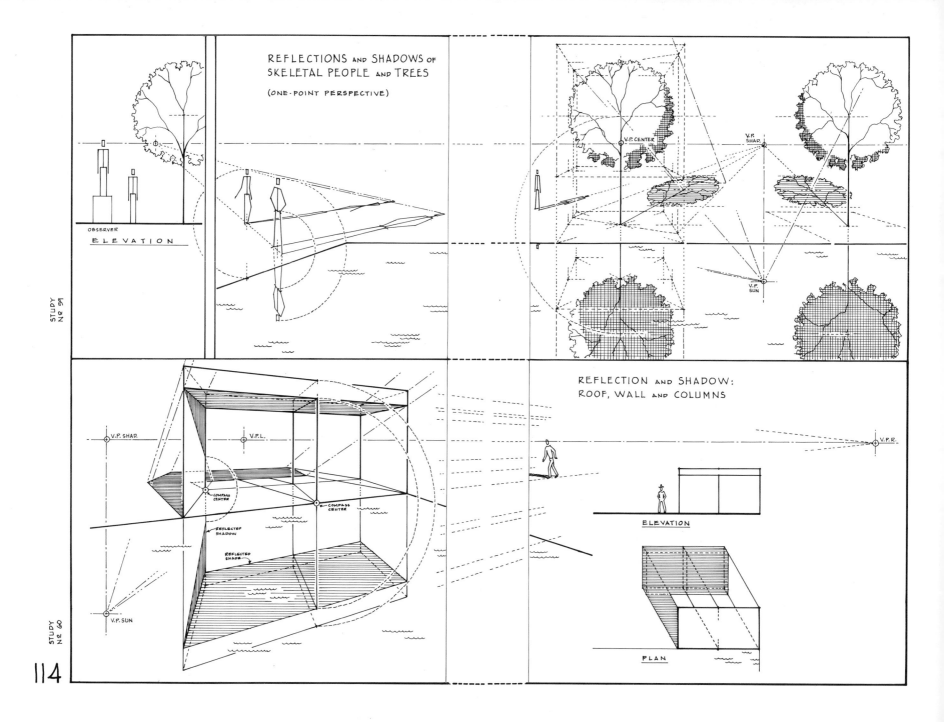

REFLECTIONS and SHADOWS of
SKELETAL PEOPLE and TREES

(ONE-POINT PERSPECTION)

OBSERVER
ELEVATION

V.P. CENTER

V.P. SHAD.

V.P. SUN

REFLECTION and SHADOW:
ROOF, WALL and COLUMNS

V.P. SHAD.

V.P.L.

V.P.R.

COMPASS CENTER

COMPASS CENTER

REFLECTED SHADOW

REFLECTED SHADE

V.P. SUN

ELEVATION

PLAN

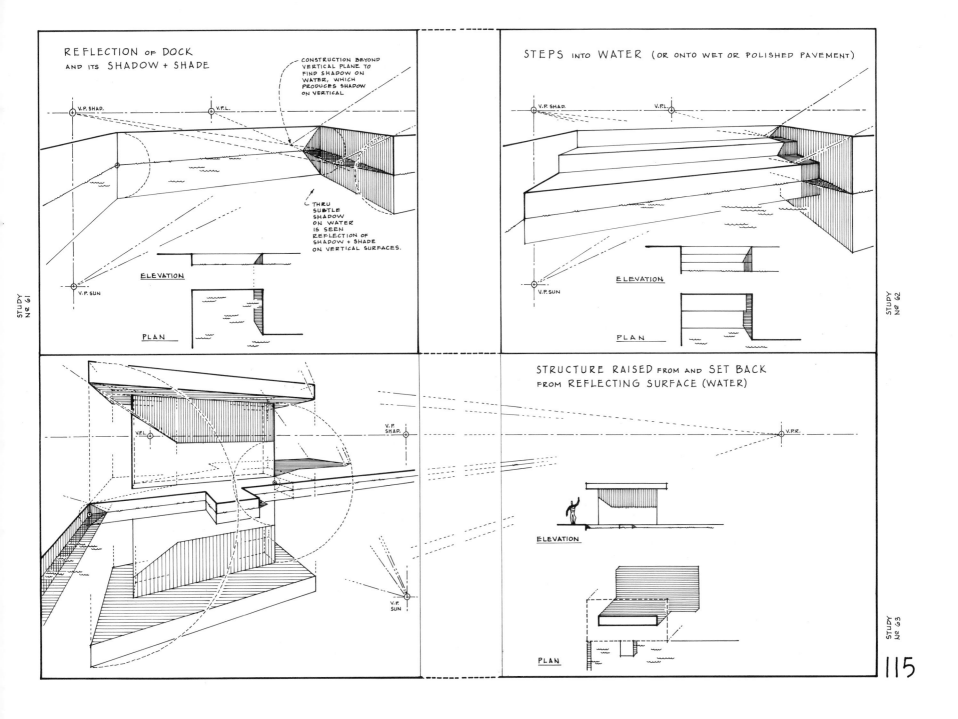

REFLECTION of DOCK
and its SHADOW + SHADE

CONSTRUCTION BEYOND
VERTICAL PLANE TO
FIND SHADOW ON
WATER, WHICH
PRODUCES SHADOW
ON VERTICAL

V.P. SHAD.

V.P.L.

THRU
SUBTLE
SHADOW
ON WATER
IS SEEN
REFLECTION OF
SHADOW + SHADE
ON VERTICAL SURFACES.

ELEVATION

PLAN

V.P. SUN

STUDY
No 61

STEPS INTO WATER (OR ONTO WET OR POLISHED PAVEMENT)

V.P. SHAD.

V.P.L.

ELEVATION

PLAN

V.P. SUN

STUDY
No 62

V.P.L.

V.P.
SHAD.

V.P.R.

V.P.
SUN

STRUCTURE RAISED FROM and SET BACK
FROM REFLECTING SURFACE (WATER)

ELEVATION

PLAN

STUDY
No 63

115

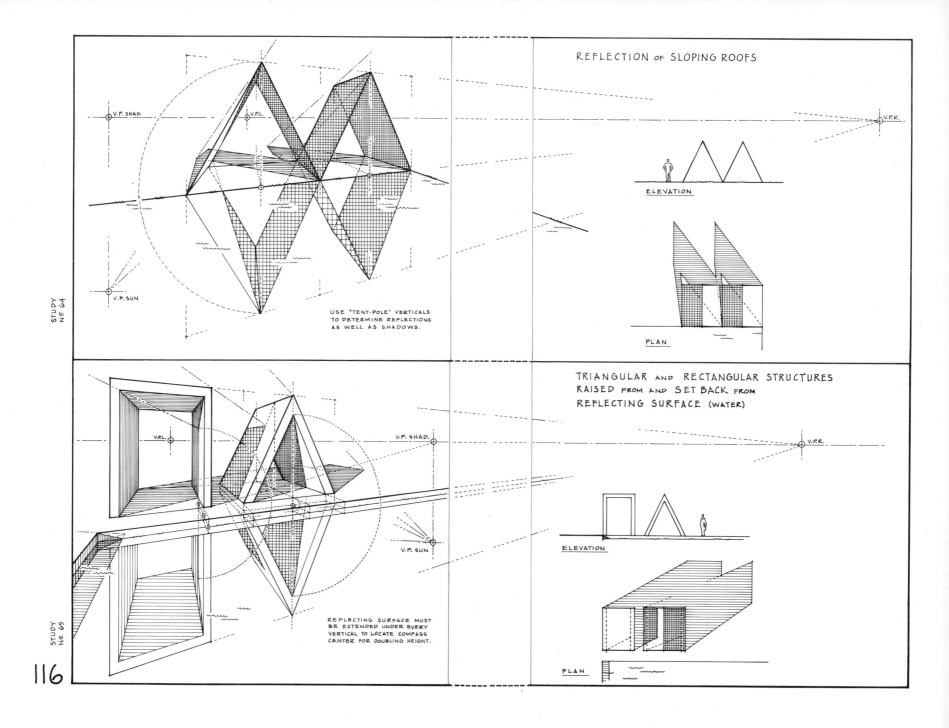

REFLECTION of SLOPING ROOFS

ELEVATION

PLAN

USE "TENT-POLE" VERTICALS
TO DETERMINE REFLECTIONS
AS WELL AS SHADOWS.

V.P. SHAD.

V.P.L.

V.P.SUN

V.P.R.

TRIANGULAR AND RECTANGULAR STRUCTURES
RAISED FROM AND SET BACK FROM
REFLECTING SURFACE (WATER)

ELEVATION

PLAN

REFLECTING SURFACE MUST
BE EXTENDED UNDER EVERY
VERTICAL TO LOCATE COMPASS
CENTER FOR DOUBLING HEIGHT.

V.P.L.

V.P. SHAD.

V.P. SUN

V.P.R.

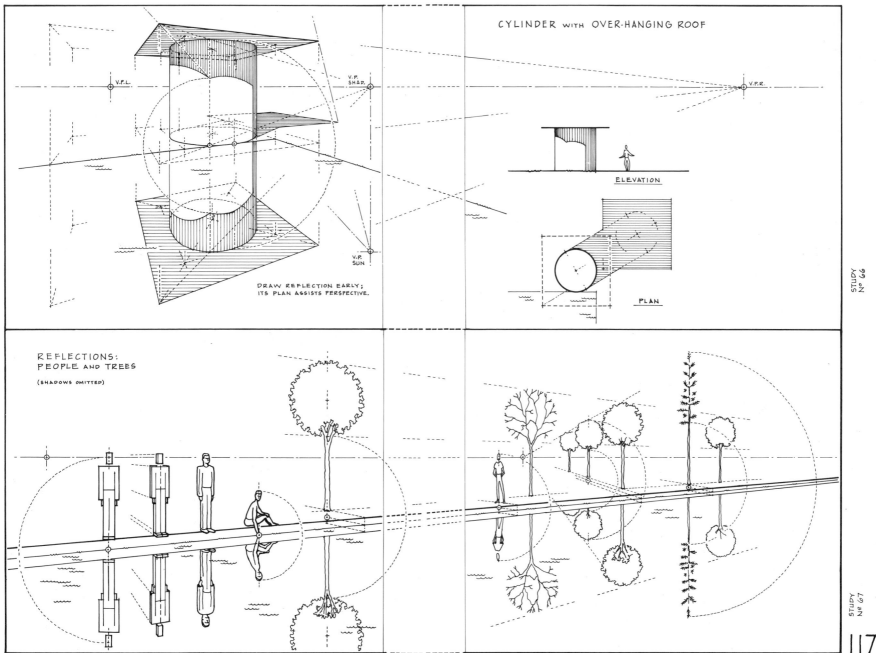

CYLINDER with OVER-HANGING ROOF

V.P.L.

V.P. SHAD.

V.P.R.

V.P. SUN

DRAW REFLECTION EARLY;
ITS PLAN ASSISTS PERSPECTIVE.

ELEVATION

PLAN

REFLECTIONS:
PEOPLE and TREES

(SHADOWS OMITTED)

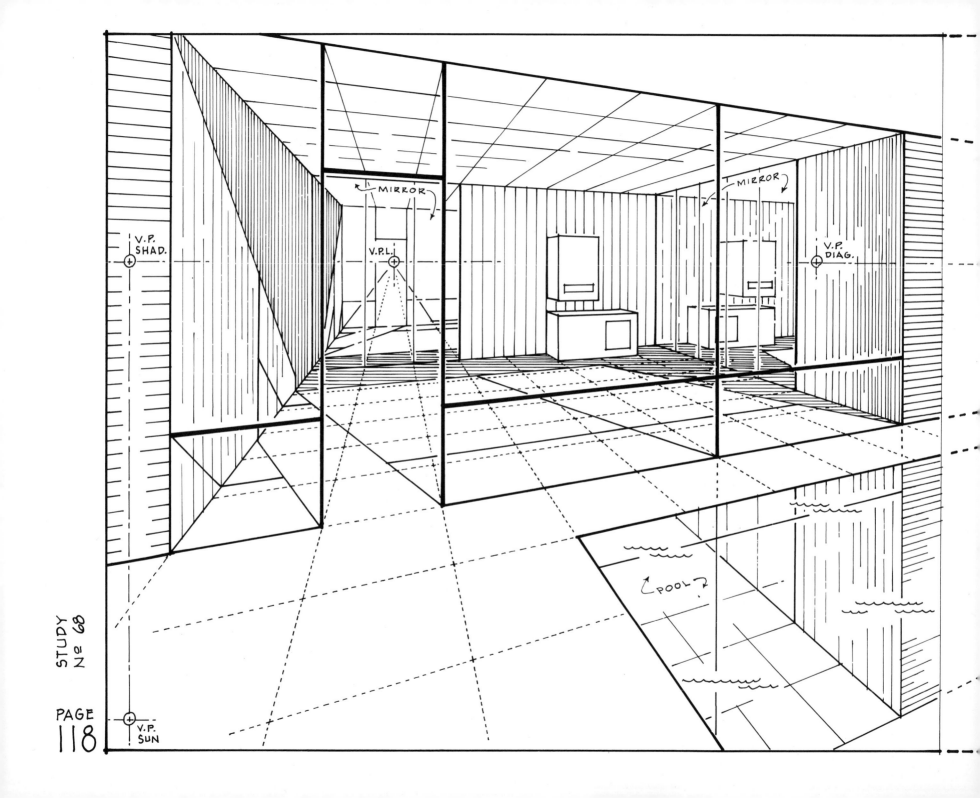

MIRROR

MIRROR

V.P.
SHAD.

V.P.L.

V.P.
DIAG.

POOL?

V.P.
SUN

MIRRORS: REFLECTIONS IN VERTICAL SURFACES

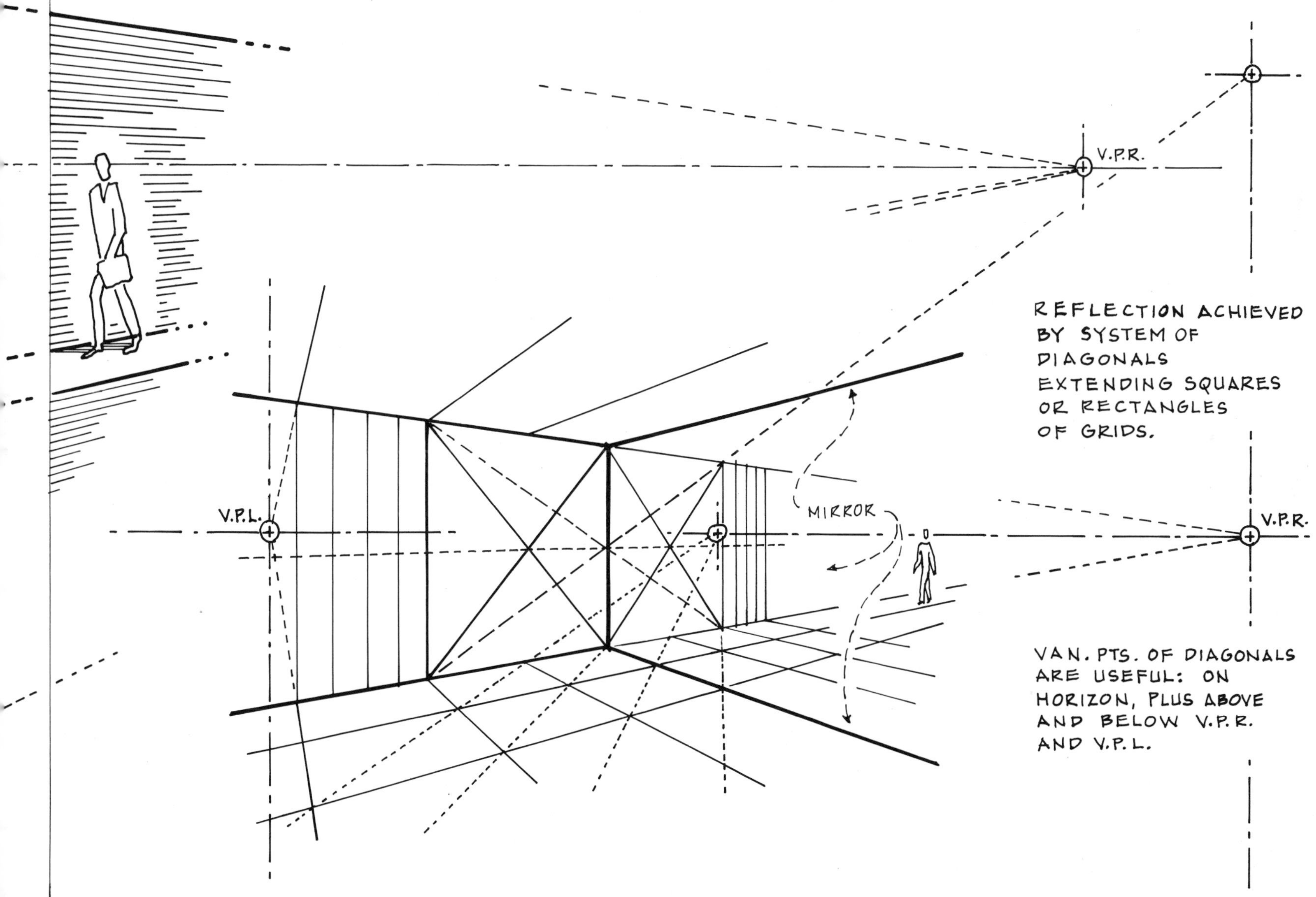

V.P.R.

V.P.R.

V.P.L.

REFLECTION ACHIEVED
BY SYSTEM OF
DIAGONALS
EXTENDING SQUARES
OR RECTANGLES
OF GRIDS.

MIRROR

VAN. PTS. OF DIAGONALS
ARE USEFUL: ON
HORIZON, PLUS ABOVE
AND BELOW V.P.R.
AND V.P.L.

MIRROR BUILDING

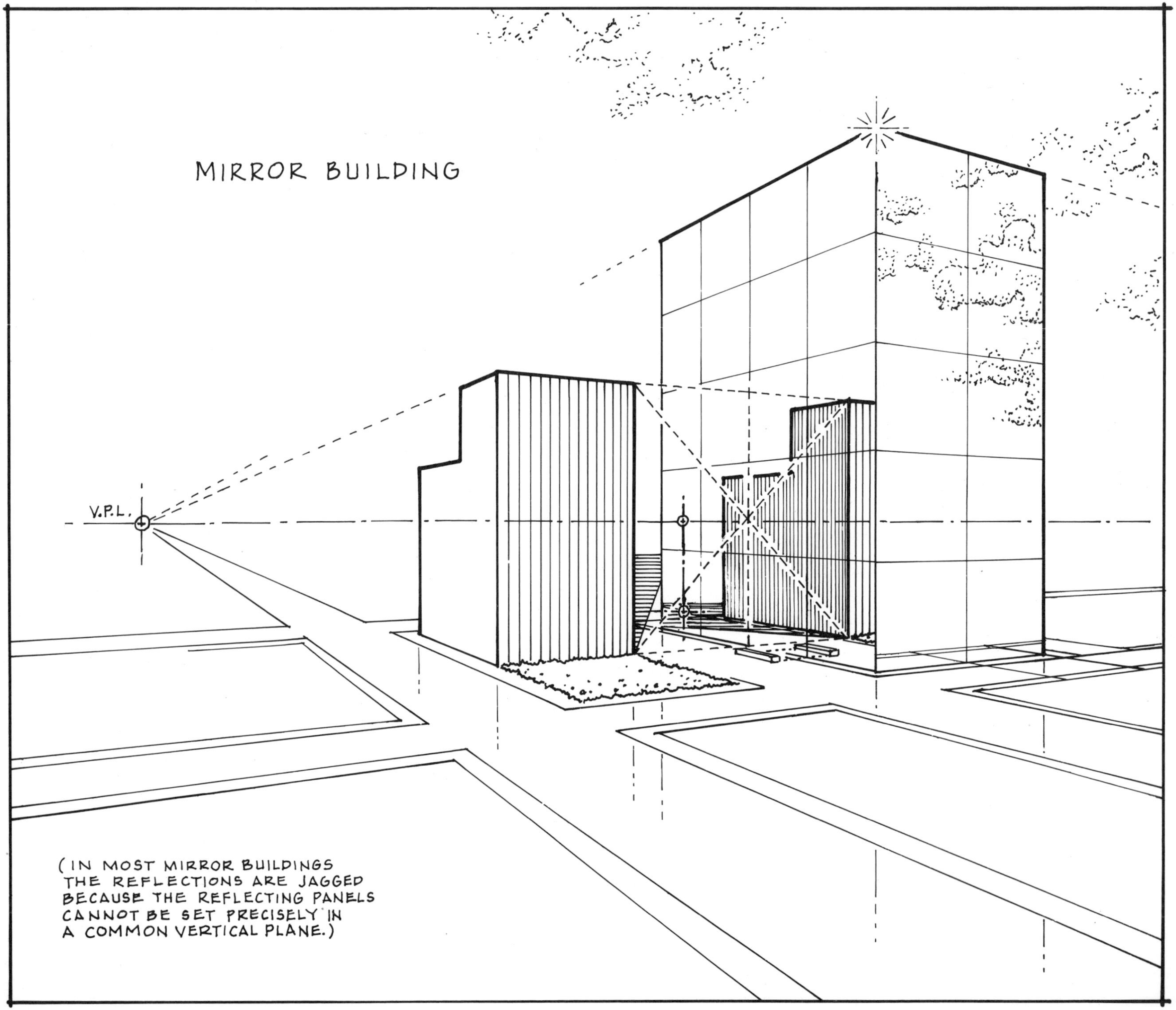

V.P.L.

(IN MOST MIRROR BUILDINGS
THE REFLECTIONS ARE JAGGED
BECAUSE THE REFLECTING PANELS
CANNOT BE SET PRECISELY IN
A COMMON VERTICAL PLANE.)

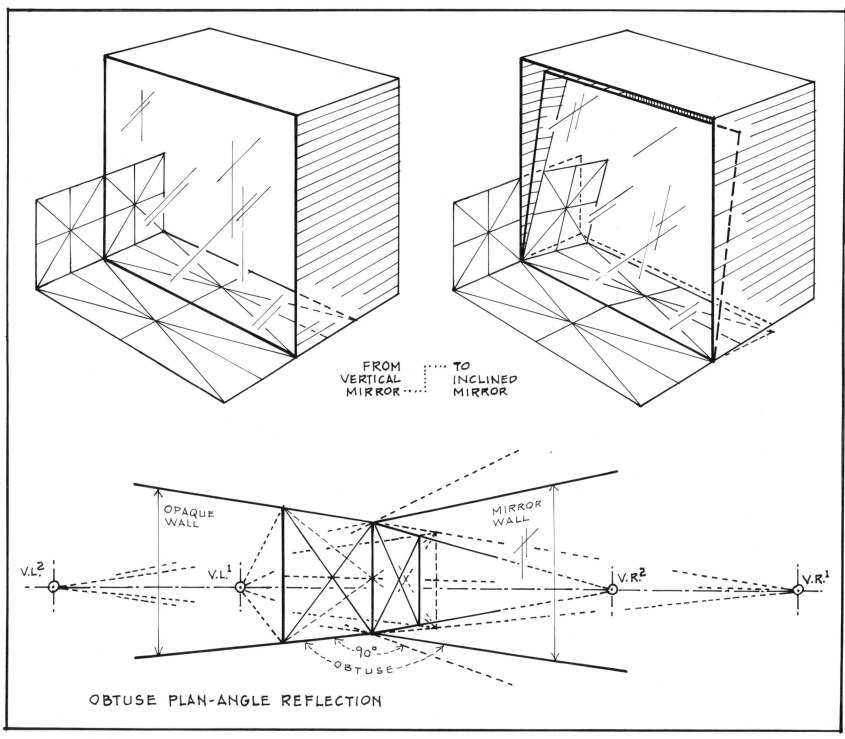

FROM
VERTICAL
MIRROR ·····

TO
INCLINED
MIRROR

OPAQUE
WALL

MIRROR
WALL

V.L.²   V.L.¹   V.R.²   V.R.¹

90°
OBTUSE

OBTUSE PLAN-ANGLE REFLECTION

EXERCISE #15

REFLECTIONS FOR 2-POINT PERSPECTIVE

CUT AWAY THE NEXT SHEET AT DASHED LINE ————————————→
TAPE THE SHEET TO YOUR DRAWING BOARD.

CONSTRUCT THE
REFLECTIONS IN
BOTH POOL AND
MIRROR, USING
THE VARIATION
ASSIGNED BY
YOUR INSTRUCTOR:
A, B, C, OR D.

EX. #15-A

DRAW AS IS.

EX. #15-B

EXCHANGE MIRROR WITH
LEFT X-PANEL (=WALL
WITH DIAGONALS).

EX. #15-C

EXCHANGE MIRROR WITH
RIGHT X-PANEL (=WALL
WITH DIAGONALS).

EX. #15-D

MAKE RIGHT X-PANEL
(=WALL WITH DIAGONALS)
ALSO A MIRROR.

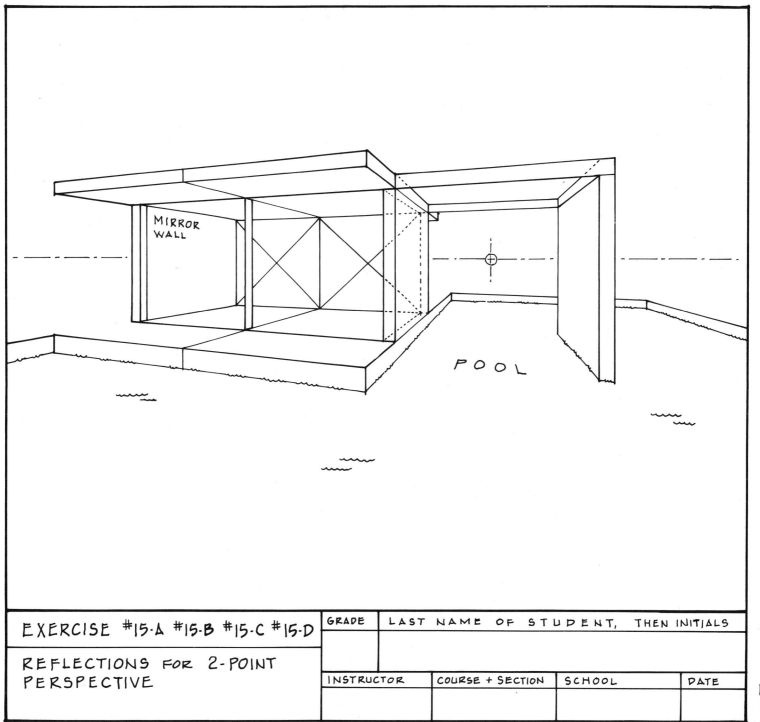

MIRROR
WALL

POOL

EXERCISE #15·A #15·B #15·C #15·D

REFLECTIONS FOR 2-POINT
PERSPECTIVE

GRADE	LAST NAME OF STUDENT, THEN INITIALS			
INSTRUCTOR	COURSE + SECTION	SCHOOL		DATE

PAGE
123

$\boxed{\text{EXERCISE \#16}}$ (DO NOT REMOVE THIS SHEET: NEW STUDY ON OTHER SIDE.)

REFLECTIONS FOR 2-POINT PERSPECTIVE

TRACE THE BUILDING OF EXERCISE #13, BUT CHANGE THE MAIN ROOF FROM FLAT TO TWO QUARTER-CIRCLE VAULTS. APPLY THE SAME-LETTER VARIATION BELOW, AND DRAW THE REFLECTIONS.

EX. #16-A

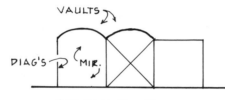

EX. #16-B

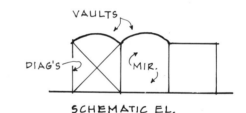

ALSO ON YOUR PAPER, COMPLETE THE TITLE BOX WITH ADJUSTED INFORMATION.

EX. #16-C

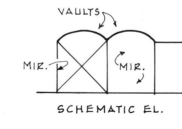

EX. #16-D

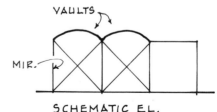

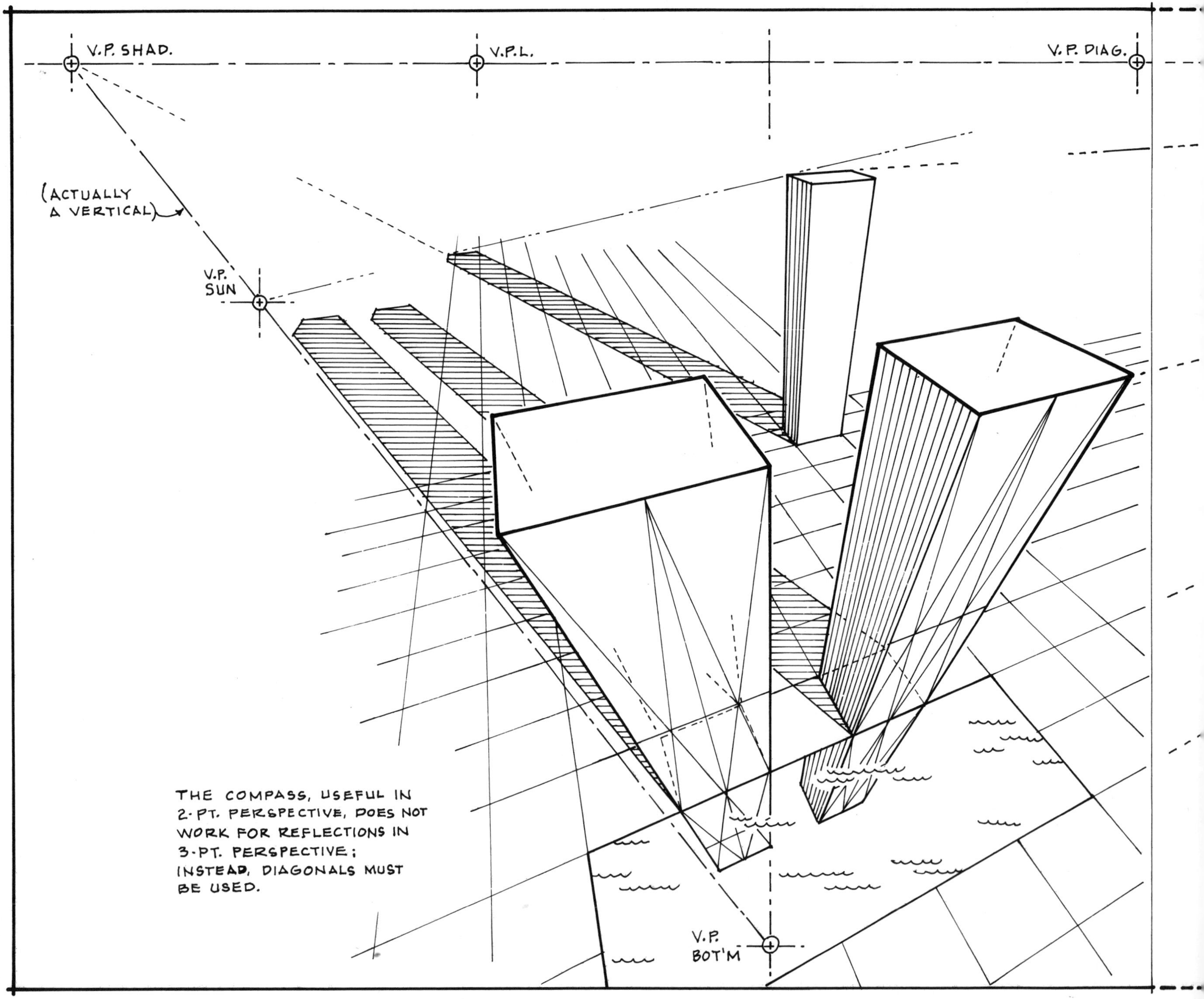

(ACTUALLY
A VERTICAL)

V.P.
SUN

THE COMPASS, USEFUL IN
2·PT. PERSPECTIVE, DOES NOT
WORK FOR REFLECTIONS IN
3·PT. PERSPECTIVE;
INSTEAD, DIAGONALS MUST
BE USED.

V.P.
BOT'M

STUDY
№ 71

PAGE
126

EXERCISE #16 (DO NOT REMOVE THIS SHEET: NEW STUDY ON OTHER SIDE.)

REFLECTIONS FOR 2-POINT PERSPECTIVE

TRACE THE BUILDING OF EXERCISE #13, BUT CHANGE THE MAIN ROOF FROM FLAT TO TWO QUARTER-CIRCLE VAULTS.   APPLY THE SAME-LETTER VARIATION BELOW, AND DRAW THE REFLECTIONS.

ALSO ON
YOUR PAPER,
COMPLETE THE
TITLE BOX
WITH ADJUSTED
INFORMATION.

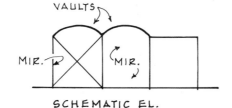

EX. #16-A

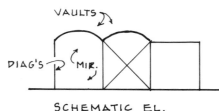

VAULTS

DIAG'S   MIR.

SCHEMATIC EL.

EX. #16-B

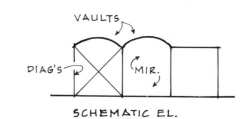

VAULTS

DIAG'S   MIR.

SCHEMATIC EL.

EX. #16-C

VAULTS

MIR.   MIR.

SCHEMATIC EL.

EX. #16-D

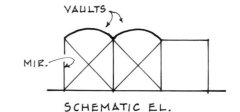

VAULTS

MIR.

SCHEMATIC EL.

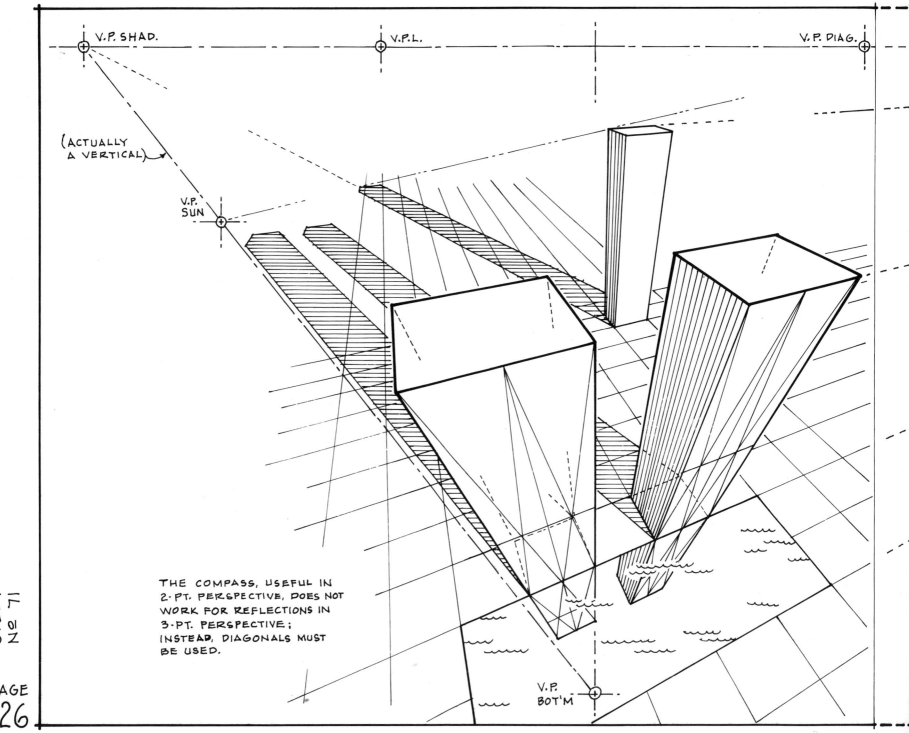

V.P. SHAD.

V.P.L.

V.P. DIAG.

(ACTUALLY A VERTICAL)

V.P. SUN

THE COMPASS, USEFUL IN
2·PT. PERSPECTIVE, DOES NOT
WORK FOR REFLECTIONS IN
3·PT. PERSPECTIVE;
INSTEAD, DIAGONALS MUST
BE USED.

V.P. BOT'M

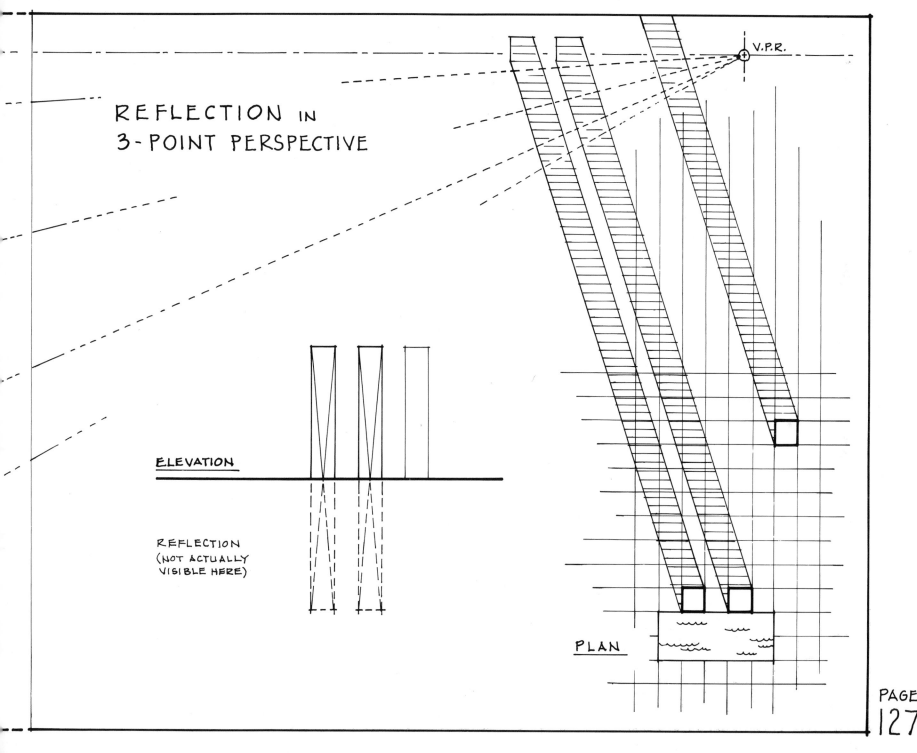

REFLECTION IN
3-POINT PERSPECTIVE

V.P.R.

ELEVATION

REFLECTION
(NOT ACTUALLY
VISIBLE HERE)

PLAN

EXERCISE #17

REFLECTIONS FOR 3-POINT PERSPECTIVE

CUT AWAY THE NEXT SHEET AT DASHED LINE ————————————→
TAPE THE SHEET TO YOUR DRAWING BOARD.

CONSTRUCT THE
REFLECTION,
USING THE
VARIATION
ASSIGNED
BY YOUR
INSTRUCTOR:
A, B, C, OR D.

EX. #17-A

CHANGE TOP THUS:

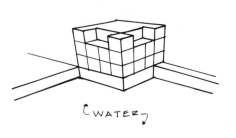

⟨WATER⟩

EX. #17-B

CHANGE TOP THUS:

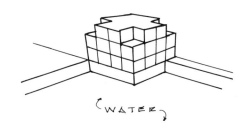

⟨WATER⟩

EX. #17-C

CHANGE TOP THUS:

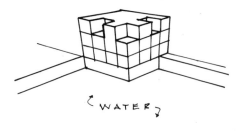

⟨WATER⟩

EX. #17-D

CHANGE TOP THUS:

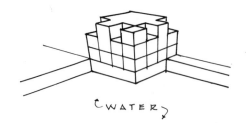

⟨WATER⟩

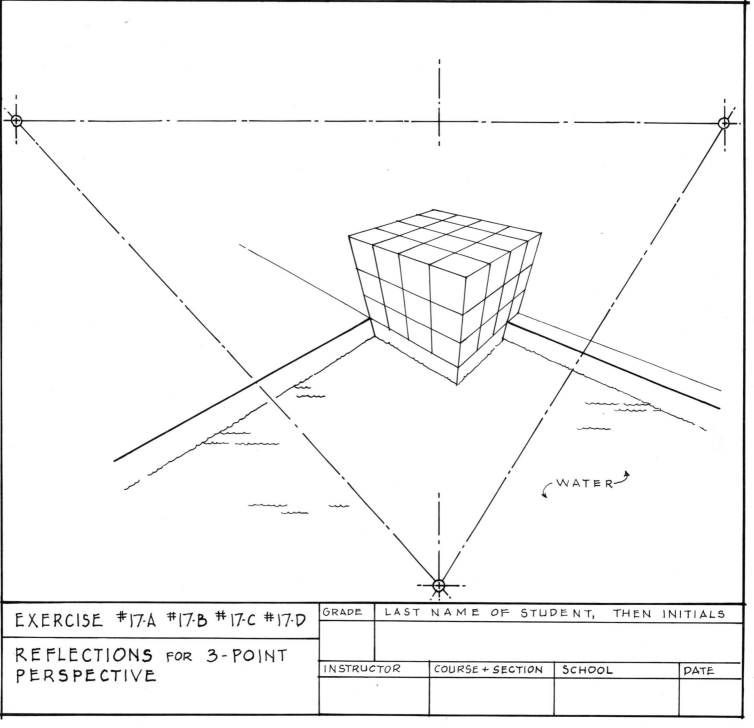

WATER

EXERCISE #17·A #17·B #17·C #17·D	GRADE	LAST NAME OF STUDENT, THEN INITIALS			
REFLECTIONS FOR 3-POINT PERSPECTIVE		INSTRUCTOR	COURSE + SECTION	SCHOOL	DATE

EXERCISE #18

(DO NOT REMOVE THIS SHEET: NEW STUDY ON OTHER SIDE.)

REFLECTIONS FOR 3-POINT PERSPECTIVE

TRACE LIGHTLY THE CUBE-MODULE FRAME OF EX.#17. EXTEND IT DOWNWARD AND MODIFY IT ACCORDING TO A, B, C, OR D, AS ASSIGNED BY INSTRUCTOR. CONSTRUCT THE REFLECTION.

ALSO ON YOUR PAPER, COMPLETE THE TITLE BOX WITH ADJUSTED INFORMATION.

EX. #18-A

PITCHED ROOFS

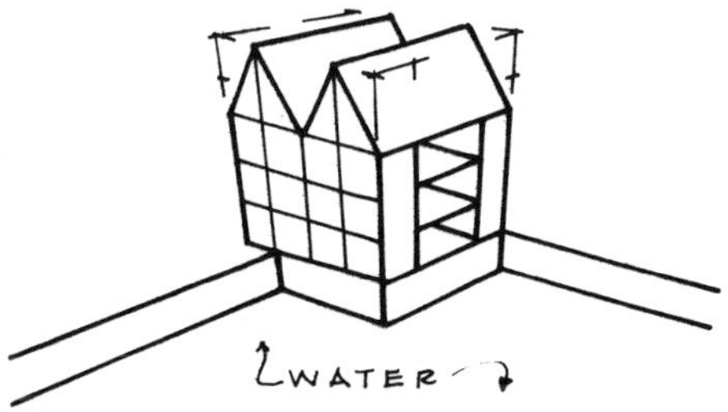
WATER

EX. #18-B

HIPPED ROOF

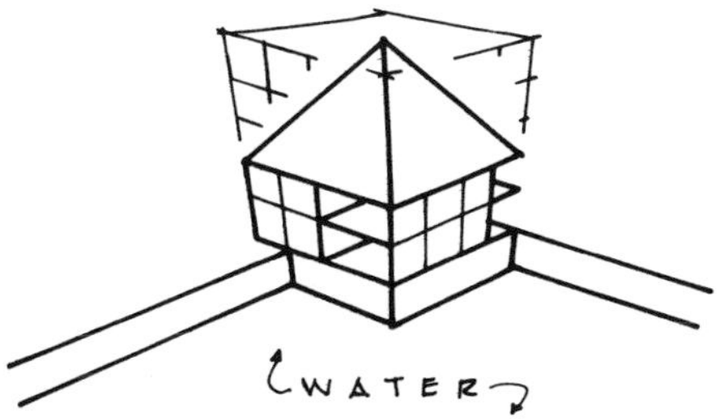
WATER

EX. #18-C

JOINED SHED ROOFS

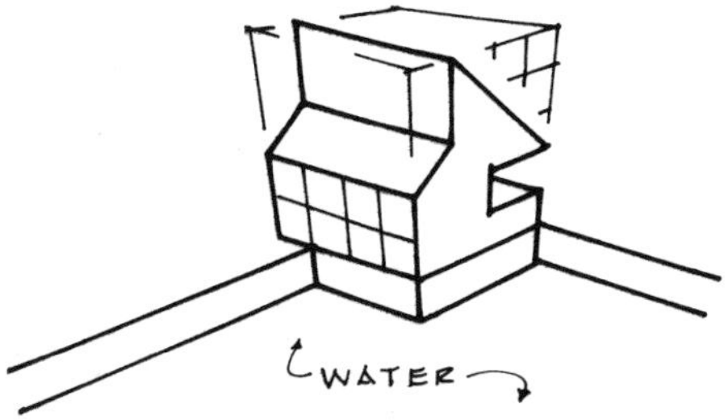
WATER

EX. #18-D

BUTTERFLY ROOF

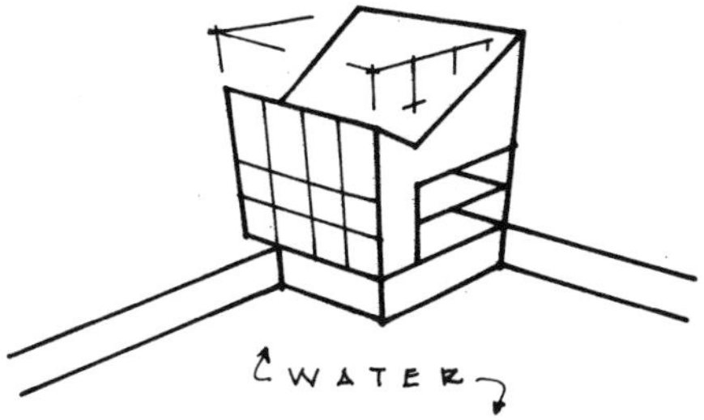
WATER

COMBINED
OVER-LAPPING
EFFECTS FOR
WINDOWS

TRANSPARENCY

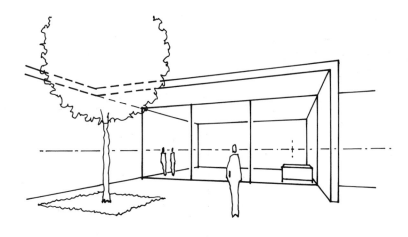

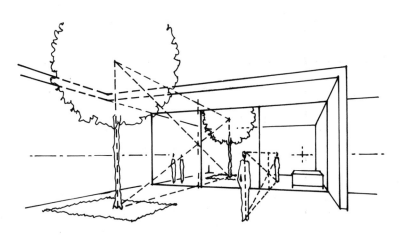

REFLECTION

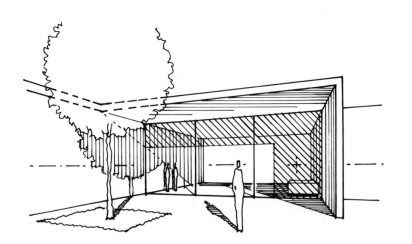

SHADOWS

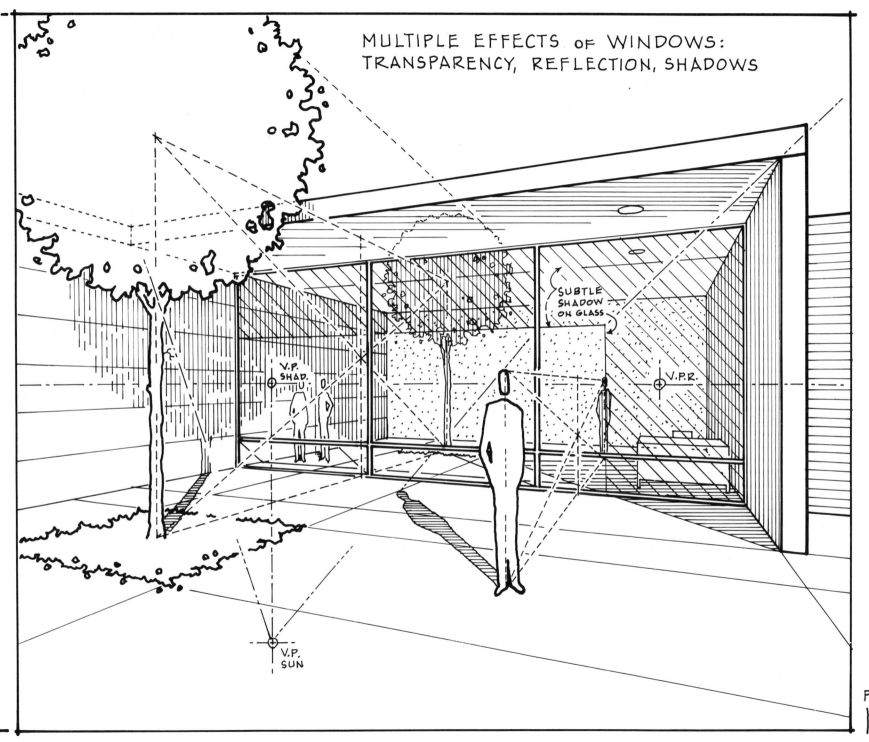

MULTIPLE EFFECTS OF WINDOWS:
TRANSPARENCY, REFLECTION, SHADOWS

SUBTLE SHADOW ON GLASS

V.P. SHAD.

V.P.R.

V.P. SUN

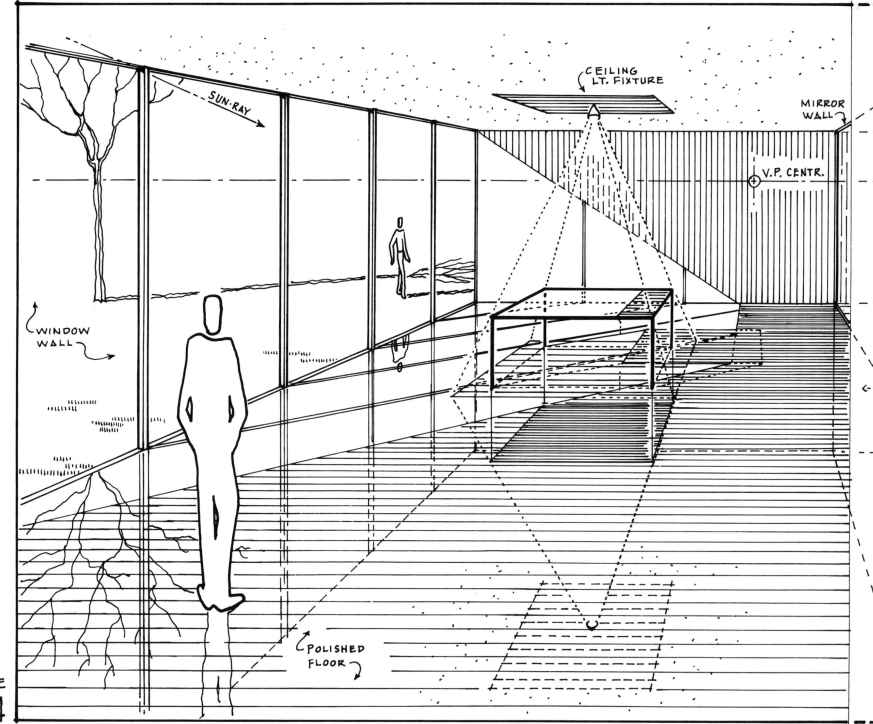

SUN·RAY

CEILING
LT. FIXTURE

MIRROR
WALL

V.P. CENTR.

WINDOW
WALL

POLISHED
FLOOR

STUDY
Nº 73

PAGE
134

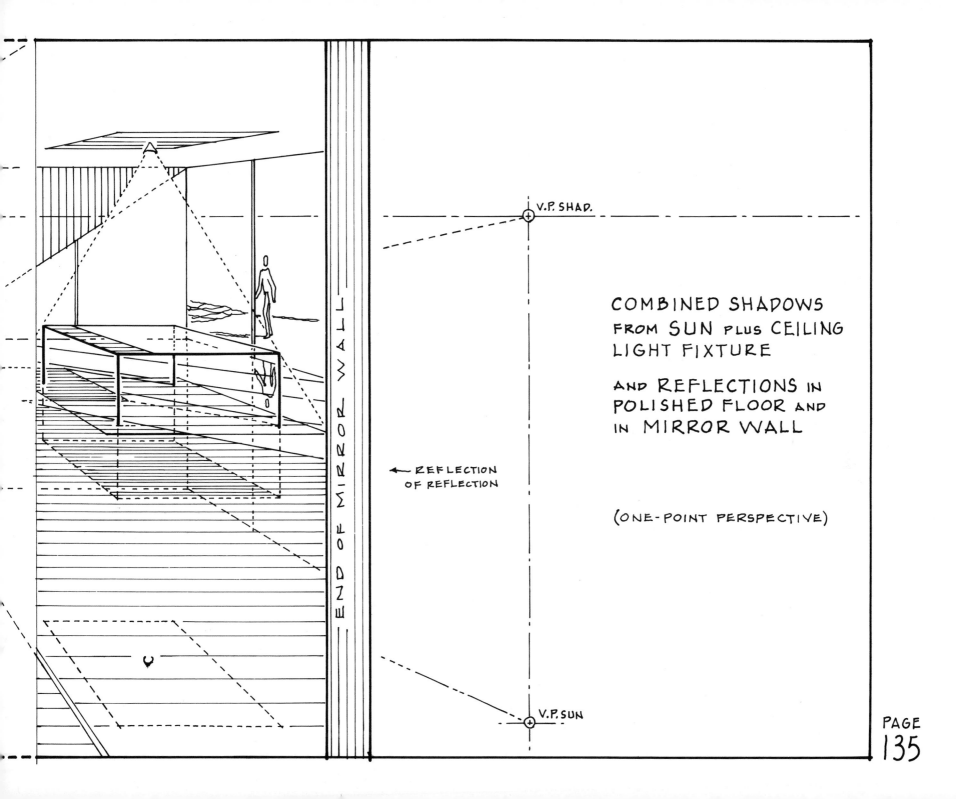

END OF MIRROR WALL

V.P. SHAD.

← REFLECTION
OF REFLECTION

COMBINED SHADOWS
FROM SUN PLUS CEILING
LIGHT FIXTURE

AND REFLECTIONS IN
POLISHED FLOOR AND
IN MIRROR WALL

(ONE-POINT PERSPECTIVE)

V.P. SUN

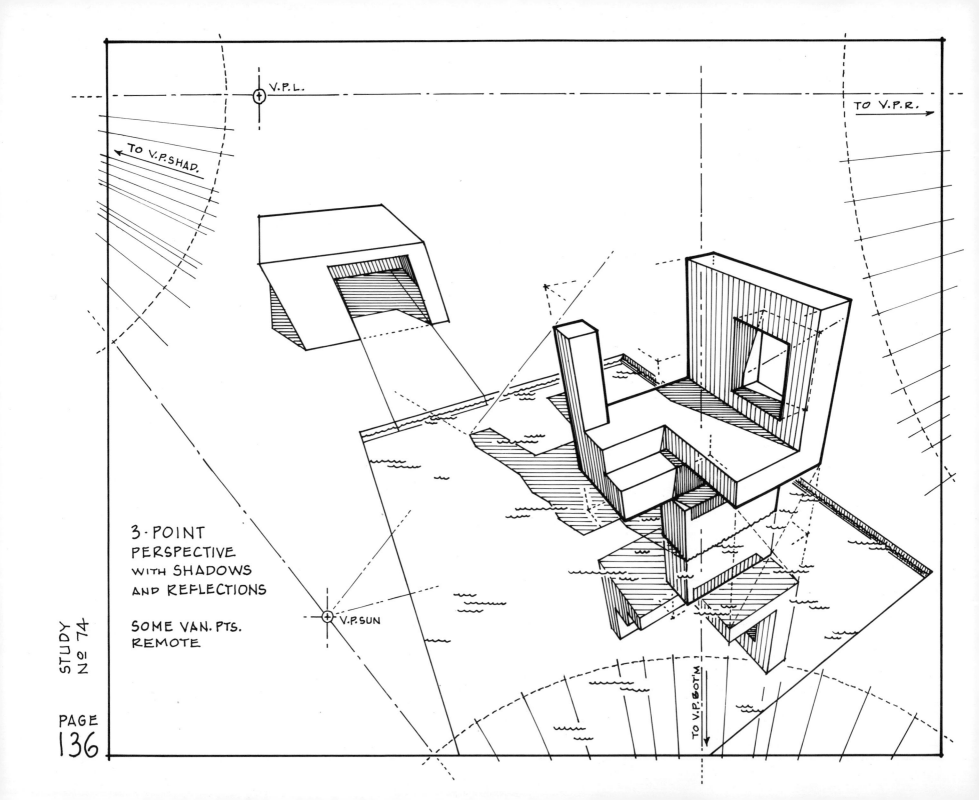

V.P.L.

TO V.P.R.

TO V.P.SHAD.

3·POINT
PERSPECTIVE
WITH SHADOWS
AND REFLECTIONS

SOME VAN. PTS.
REMOTE

V.P. SUN

TO V.P. BOT'M

STUDY
N⁰ 74

PAGE
136

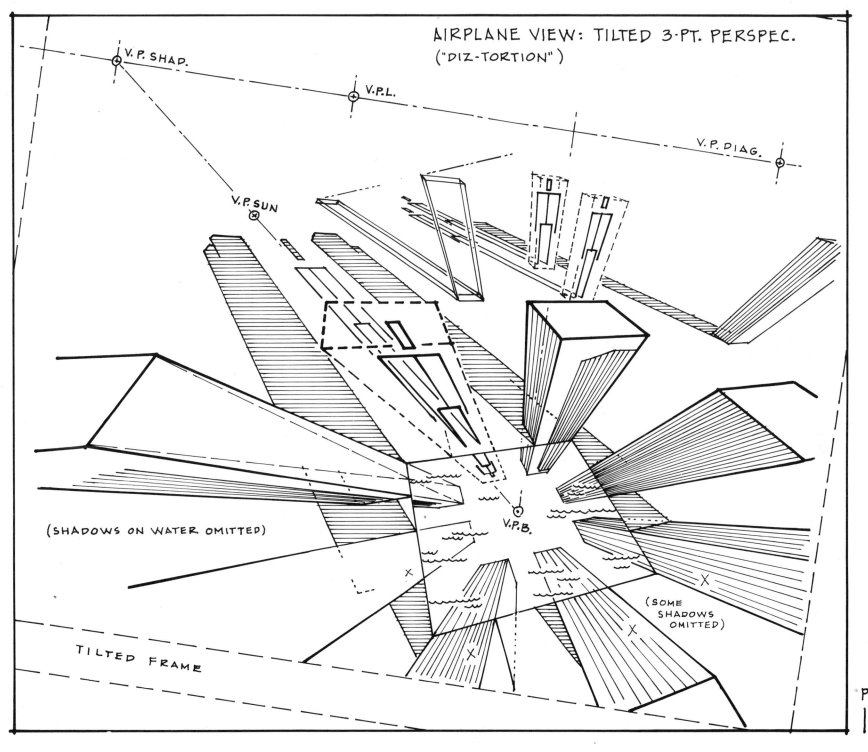

AIRPLANE VIEW: TILTED 3-PT. PERSPEC.
("DIZ-TORTION")

V.P. SHAD.

V.P.L.

V.P. DIAG.

V.P. SUN

(SHADOWS ON WATER OMITTED)

V.P.B.

(SOME SHADOWS OMITTED)

TILTED FRAME

STUDY № 75

PAGE 137

EXERCISE #19

SHADOWS + REFLECTIONS FOR 2-POINT PERSPECTIVE

CUT AWAY THE NEXT SHEET AT DASHED LINE ⟶
TAPE THE SHEET TO YOUR DRAWING BOARD.

USING A, B, C, OR D
AS ASSIGNED BY
YOUR INSTRUCTOR,
FIRST, FIND
VANISHING POINT
FOR SHADOWS;
SECOND, FIND
VANISHING POINT
FOR SUN-RAYS;
THIRD, CONSTRUCT
ALL SHADOWS.

USE SPACED-LINE
TEXTURE FOR
SHADE AND
SHADOW.

FOURTH, CONSTRUCT
THE REFLECTION.

SHOW REFLECTED
TEXTURES.

EX. #19-A

USE SUN-RAY A, CASTING
SHADOW OF ROOF CORNER
AT POINT A ON WALL.

EX. #19-B

USE SUN-RAY B, CASTING
SHADOW OF ROOF CORNER
AT POINT B ON WALL.

EX. #19-C

USE SUN-RAY C, CASTING
SHADOW OF ROOF CORNER
AT POINT C ON WALL.

EX. #19-D

USE SUN-RAY D, CASTING
SHADOW OF ROOF CORNER
AT POINT D ON WALL.

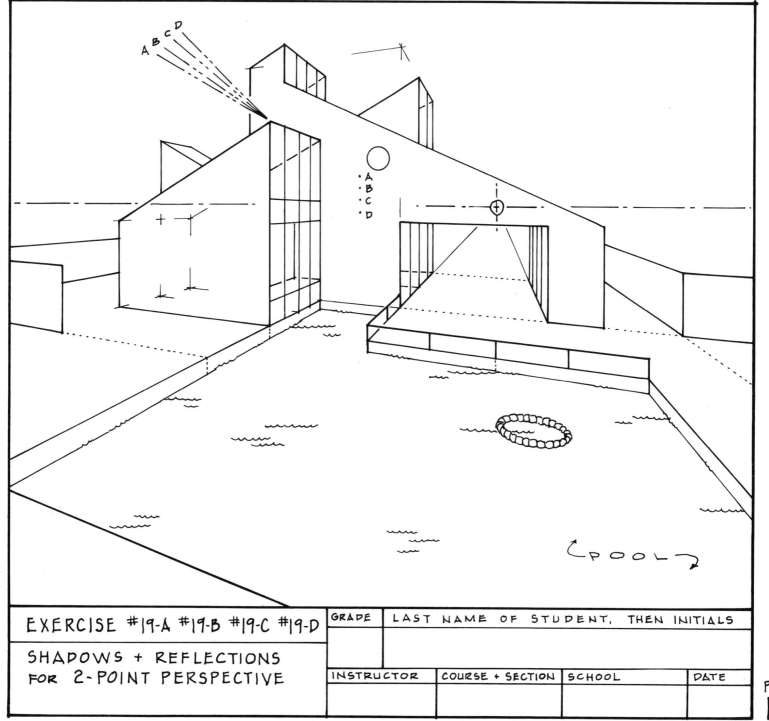

A B C D

·A
·B
·C
·D

⌐POOL⌐

EXERCISE #19-A #19-B #19-C #19-D	GRADE	LAST NAME OF STUDENT, THEN INITIALS			
SHADOWS + REFLECTIONS FOR 2-POINT PERSPECTIVE					
	INSTRUCTOR	COURSE + SECTION	SCHOOL		DATE

PAGE
139

EXERCISE #20 (DO NOT REMOVE THIS SHEET: NEW STUDY ON OTHER SIDE.)

SHADOWS + REFLECTIONS FOR 3-POINT PERSPECTIVE

CONVERT EX.#19 TO A 3-POINT PERSPECTIVE (AERIAL), USING AN APPROPRIATE CUBE-MODULE FRAME. CONSTRUCT SHADOWS AND REFLECTION.

EX. #20-A INDIVIDUAL	EX. #20-B INDIVIDUAL
EX. 20-C INDIVIDUAL	EX. 20-D INDIVIDUAL

ALSO ON YOUR PAPER, COMPLETE THE TITLE BOX WITH ADJUSTED INFORMATION.

VEHICLES:
REFLECTIONS and SHADOWS

(ONE·PT. PERSPEC.)

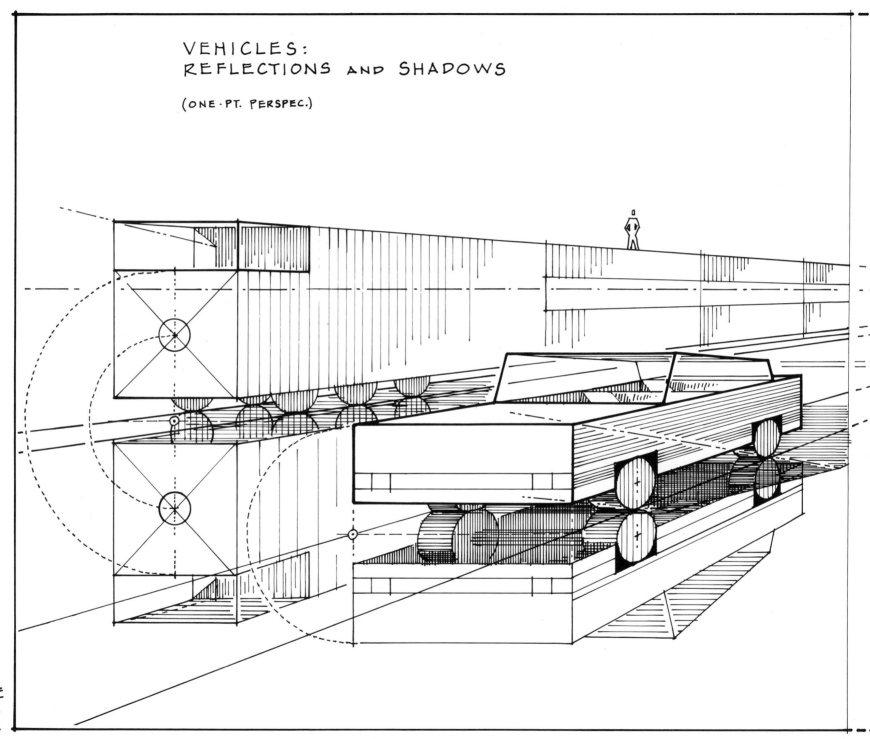

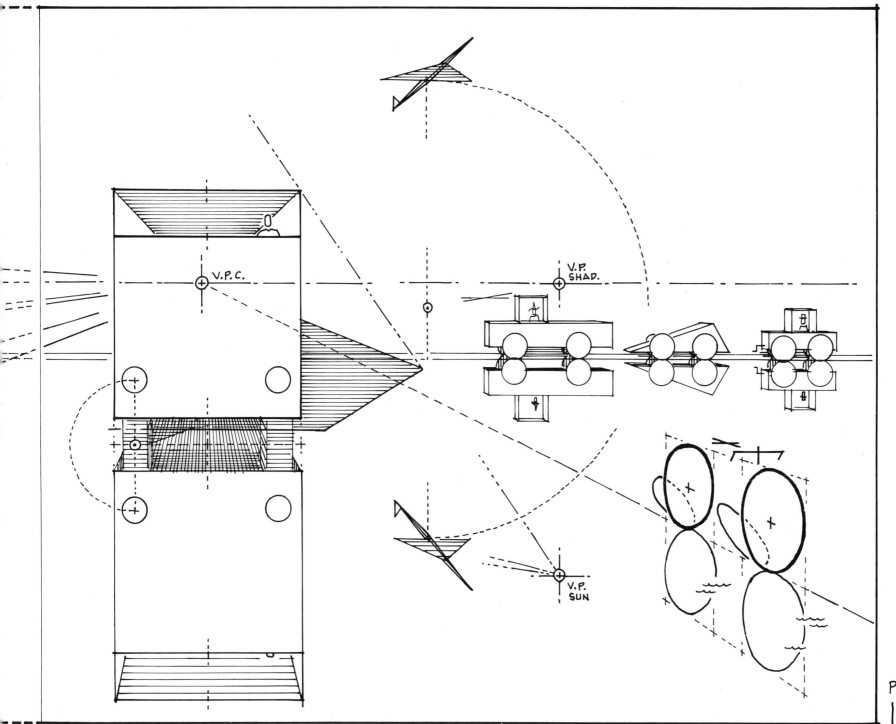

V.P.C.

V.P.
SHAD.

V.P.
SUN

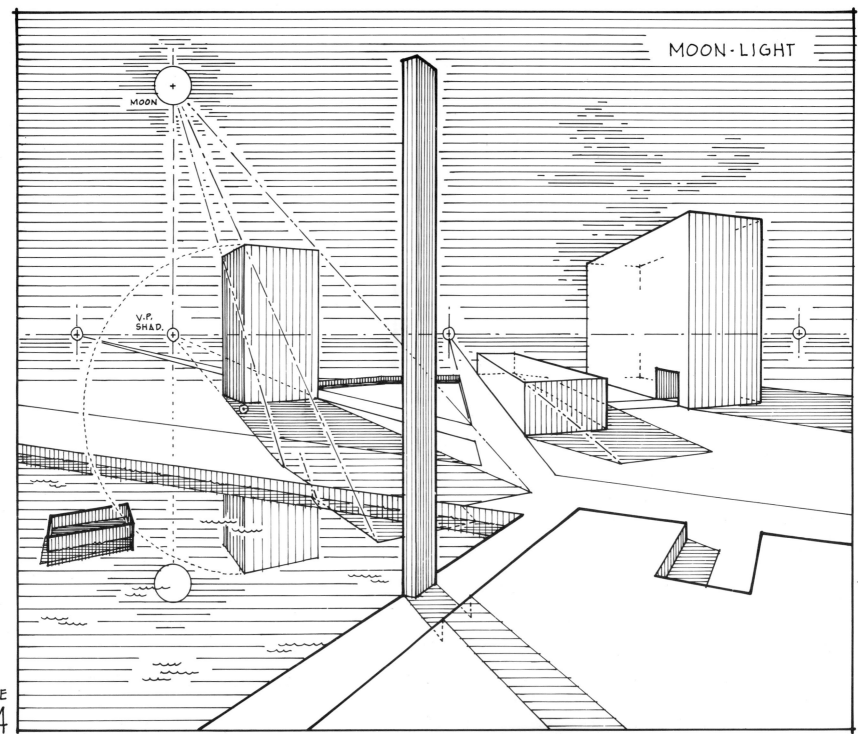

MOON·LIGHT

MOON

V.P.
SHAD.

RAIN·LIGHT

SCHOOL OF ARCHITECTURE, DACCA, BANGLADESH
ARCHITECT: DIK VROMAN

STUDY Nº 78

PAGE
145

TEXTURES OF MATERIALS: LIGHT, SHADE, SHADOW, REFLECTION

① OUTLINE OF SHAD. + REFLEC.

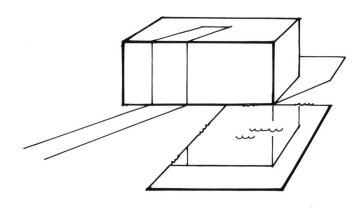

② ARBITRARY TEXTURES = CONSTR. DRWG.

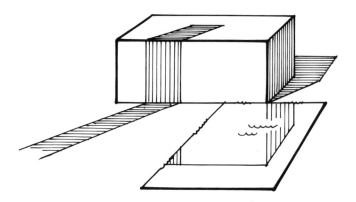

③ REAL TEXTURES IN SHAD. ONLY

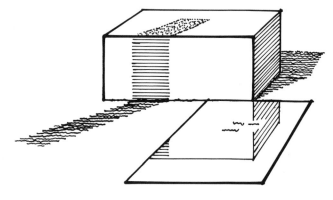

④ ALL TEXTURES: LT. + SHAD.

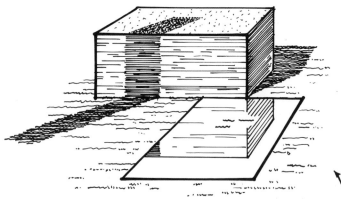

TEXTURE MUST NOT CHANGE CHARACTER IN SHAPE AND SHADOW, OR IT WILL LOOK LIKE A DIFFERENT MATERIAL OVER-LAID.

NOTE: IN THE ABOVE TWO DRWGS., #3 + 4, NO HARD OUTLINE IS USED IN THE FINISHED SHADOW RENDERING; RATHER, THE TEXTURES PROVIDE THEIR OWN OUTLINES.

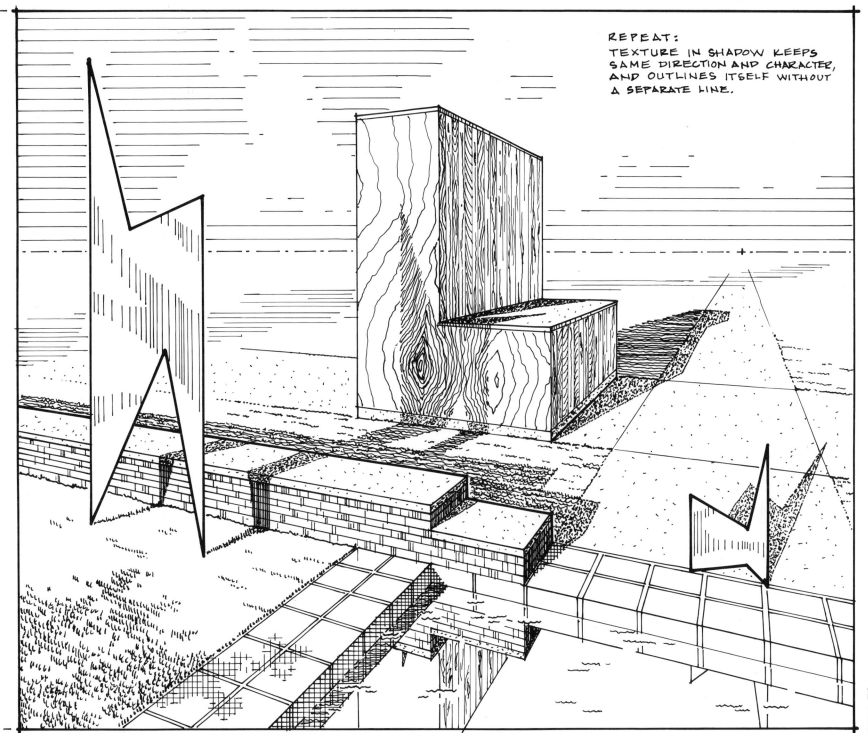

REPEAT:
TEXTURE IN SHADOW KEEPS
SAME DIRECTION AND CHARACTER,
AND OUTLINES ITSELF WITHOUT
A SEPARATE LINE.

TRANSITIONAL DRAWING:
FROM CONSTRUCTION TOWARD RENDERING

PANORAMIC VIEW
(STRETCHED WIDTH)

HORIZON LINE
DISAPPEARS IN
SUBTLE BACKGROUND

STUDY
Nº 80

STUDY
Nº 81

INTERIOR
TO EXTERIOR

148

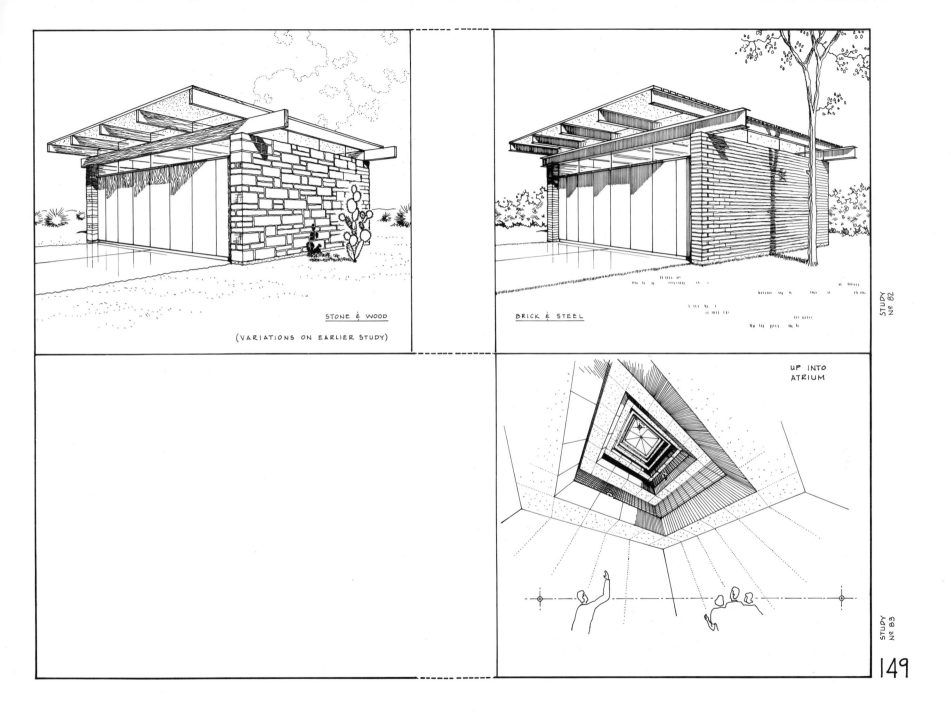

STONE & WOOD

(VARIATIONS ON EARLIER STUDY)

BRICK & STEEL

UP INTO
ATRIUM

RECTILINEAR DESIGN SKETCHED AS CURVILINEAR. SUBSTITUTES CURVILINEAR INTERPRETATION
FOR THE USUAL DISTORTION. ONE-POINT PERSPECTIVE BECOMES 5-POINT PERSPECTIVE.

(A MORE DIFFICULT WAY TO CONSTRUCT A DETAILED DRAWING, BUT A NATURAL WAY TO
SKETCH WHAT WE SEEM TO SEE)

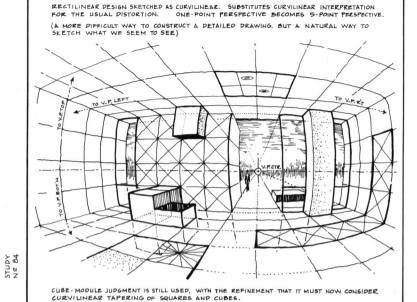

CUBE-MODULE JUDGMENT IS STILL USED, WITH THE REFINEMENT THAT IT MUST NOW CONSIDER
CURVILINEAR TAPERING OF SQUARES AND CUBES.

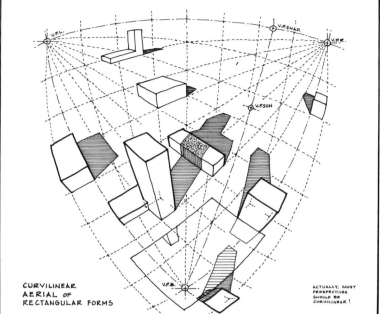

CURVILINEAR
AERIAL of
RECTANGULAR FORMS

ACTUALLY, MOST
PERSPECTIVES
SHOULD BE
CURVILINEAR!

FREE-HAND SKETCH OF A CURVILINEAR IDEA
DONE WITHOUT MECHANICS
— BUT WITH A SENSE OF
PICTURE OF A
DESIGN CONCEPT
STILL IN FIRST
THOUGHTS

IN THE LONG
RUN, THE
ABILITY WE
HOPE TO
DEVELOP IS
FREE-HAND
SKETCHING IN
PERSPECTIVE
AS A MEANS
OF EXPRESSING
DESIGN IDEAS
WHICH ARE
EVOLVING IN
OUR MINDS.

MECHANICAL
DEVICES
SHOULD REMAIN
TOOLS; THEY
SHOULD NOT
BECOME MASTERS
WHICH DIRECT
OUR DESIGNS.
LET THE EYE
AND THE HAND DO
THE DESIGNING.
SEEK THE PROPER
COMBINATION OF
FREE-HAND AND
MECHANICAL
MEANS OF
PRESENTATION.
ABOVE ALL, PUT
FEELING INTO
THE PICTURE.